ATTIC   RED-FIGURED   POTTERY

ATTIC RED-FIGURED POTTERY

by

ROBERT S. FOLSOM

NOYES CLASSICAL STUDIES

NOYES PRESS
PARK RIDGE, NEW JERSEY

Copyright © 1976 by Robert S. Folsom
Library of Congress Catalog Card Number 76-41132
ISBN: 0-8155-5049-9

Published in the United States by
NOYES PRESS
Noyes Building
Park Ridge, New Jersey 07656

Library of Congress Cataloging in Publication Data

Folsom, Robert Slade.
   Attic red-figured pottery.

   (Noyes classical studies)
   Bibliography: p.
   Includes index.
   1. Vases, Greek. 2. Vase-painting, Greek.
I. Title.
NK4649.F64   738.3′82′0938   76-41132
ISBN 0-8155-5049-9

CONTENTS

LIST OF PLATES AND FIGURES

PLATES

In selecting photographs for this book, I have chosen those which are representative of the great masters and those which best illustrate developments in styles of vase painting. In general, this has meant selection of masterpieces which have often been shown before. However, where possible, I have used less well-known vases to provide variety.

13. Rf Nikosthenic amphora: Ht. 38.5 cm., by Oltos, ca. 525–510 B.C., Louvre G 2.
    Photo: Hirmer Fotoarchiv München.

14. Rf kylix: Ht. 13.5 cm., diam. 33.0 cm., by Epiktetos, ca. 520 B.C., London E 3.
    Photo: The British Museum.

15. Tondo of the preceding kylix.
    Photo: The British Museum.

16. Rf amphora: Ht. 69 cm., by the Berlin Painter, ca. 500–480 B.C., Berlin F 2160.
    Photo: Hirmer Fotoarchiv München.

17. Rf bell-krater: Ht. 33 cm., by the Berlin Painter, ca. 490 B.C., Louvre G 175.
    Photo: Hirmer Fotoarchiv München.

18. Rf amphora: Ht. 41.6 cm., by the Berlin Painter, ca. 490 B.C., New York 56.171.38.
    Photo: The Metropolitan Museum of Art, New York.

19. Rf calyx-krater: Ht. 43.8 cm., by the Kleophrades Painter, ca. 490–480 B.C.., Fogg 1960.236.
    Photo: The Fogg Art Museum, Harvard University, Cambridge.

20. Rf neck-amphora: Ht. 56 cm., by the Kleophrades Painter, ca. 500–490 B.C., Munich 2344.
    Photo: Hirmer Fotoarchiv München.

21. Rf column-krater: Ht. 36.7 cm., by Myson, ca. 490–480 B.C., New York 56.171.45.
    Photo: The Metropolitan Museum of Art, New York.

22. Rf kylix: Diam. 24.8 cm., by Onesimos, early fifth century B.C., Boston 10.179.
    Photo: The Museum of Fine Arts, Boston.

23. Rf kylix: Ht. 9 cm., diam. 24.2 cm., by Onesimos, ca. 480 B.C., Brussels A 889.
    Photo: Hirmer Fotoarchiv München.

24. Rf kantharos: Ht. 24.7 cm., by the Brygos Painter, early fifth century B.C., Boston 95.36.
    Photo: The Museum of Fine Arts, Boston.

25. Rf kylix: Ht. 12.4 cm., diam. 27.4 cm., by the Brygos Painter, ca. 490–480 B.C., London E 65.
    Photo: The British Museum, London.

26. Rf skyphos: Ht. 21.5 cm., by Makron, ca. 490–480 B.C., Boston 13.186.
    Photo: The Museum of Fine Arts, Boston.

27. Rf kylix: Ht. 8.8 cm., diam. 19.5 cm., by Makron, ca. 490 B.C., New York 96.9.191. GR 1120.
    Photo: The Metropolitan Museum of Art, New York.

28. Rf psykter: Ht. 29 cm., by Douris, ca. 480–470 B.C., London E 768.
   Photo: The British Museum, London.

29. Rf kylix: Ht. 12 cm., diam. 26.5 cm., by Douris, ca. 495–480 B.C., Louvre G 115.
   Photo: Hirmer Fotoarchiv München.

30. Rf kylix: Ht. 11.1 cm., diam. 29.9 cm., by Douris, ca. 480–470 B.C., New York 52.11.4.
   Photo: The Metropolitan Museum of Art, New York.

31. Rf bell-krater: Ht. 37.5 cm., by the Pan Painter, ca. 470 B.C., Boston 10.185.
   Photo: The Museum of Fine Arts, Boston.

32. Rf neck-amphora: Ht. 39.5 cm., by the Pan Painter, ca. 460 B.C., New York 20.245.
   Photo: The Metropolitan Museum of Art, New York.

33. Rf lekythos: Ht. 31.4 cm., by the Pan Painter, ca. 470–460 B.C., Boston 01.8079.
   Photo: The Museum of Fine Arts, Boston.

34. Rf column-krater: Ht. 39.4 cm., by the Pig Painter, ca. 475–450 B.C., Cleveland 24.197.
   Photo: The Cleveland Museum of Art, Cleveland.

35. Rf calyx-krater: Ht. 54 cm., by the Niobid Painter, ca. 455–450 B.C., Louvre MNC 511 (G 341).
   Photo: Hirmer Fotoarchiv München.

36. Rf bell-krater: Ht. 36.8 cm., by the Villa Giulia Painter, ca. 460–450 B.C., New York 24.97.96.
   Photo: The Metropolitan Museum of Art, New York.

37. Rf skyphos: Ht. 15 cm., by the Pistoxenos Painter, ca. 470 B.C., Schwerin 708.
   Photo: Hirmer Fotoarchiv München.

38. Rf kylix: Ht. 7.3 cm., diam. 43 cm., by the Penthesileia Painter, ca. 455 B.C., Munich 2688.
   Photo: Hirmer Fotoarchiv München.

39. Rf stamnos: Ht. 35.8 cm., by Hermonax, ca. 460 B.C., Boston 01.8031.
   Photo: The Museum of Fine Arts, Boston.

40. Rf stamnos: Ht. 40.8 cm., by Polygnotos, ca. 440 B.C., London 96.7-16.5.
   Photo: The British Museum, London.

41. Rf amphora: Ht. 60 cm., by the Achilles Painter, ca. 445–440 B.C., Vatican from Vulci.
   Photo: Hirmer Fotoarchiv München.

42. Rf neck-amphora, Nolan type: Ht. 33.8 cm., by the Achilles Painter, ca. 460–450 B.C., New York 12.236.2.
   Photo: The Metropolitan Museum of Art, New York.

43. Rf loutrophoros: Ht. 92.7 cm., by the Achilles Painter and the Sabouroff Painter, ca. 440 B.C., Philadelphia 30.4.1.
   Photo: The University Museum, University of Pennsylvania, Phila-delphia.

44. Rf oinochoe: Ht. 33.3 cm., by the Mannheim Painter, ca. 450 B.C., New York 06.1021.189.
   Photo: The Metropolitan Museum of Art, New York.

45. Rf squat lekythos: Ht. 9 cm., by the Eretria Painter, ca. 430 B.C., New York 30.11.8.
   Photo: The Metropolitan Museum of Art, New York.

46. White-ground pyxis: Ht. 14.3 cm., by the Penthesileia Painter, ca. 465–460 B.C., New York 07.286.36.
   Photo: The Metropolitan Museum of Art, New York.

47. White-ground lekythos: Ht. 38.4 cm., by the Achilles Painter, ca. 440 B.C., Boston 13.201.
   Photo: The Museum of Fine Arts, Boston.

48. White-ground lekythos: Ht. 39.4 cm., by the Achilles Painter, ca. 440 B.C., New York 07.286.42.
   Photo: The Metropolitan Museum of Art, New York.

49. White-ground lekythos: Ht. 38.6 cm., probably by the Bosanquet Painter, ca. 440–430 B.C., New York 23.160.38.
   Photo: The Metropolitan Museum of Art, New York.

50. White-ground lekythos: Ht. 48.8 cm., by the Thanatos Painter, ca. 440–435 B.C., London D 58.
   Photo: The British Museum, London.

51. White-ground lekythos: Ht. 30.1 cm., by the Bird Painter, ca. 450–430 B.C., Fogg 1925.30.54.
   Photo: The Fogg Art Museum, Harvard University, Cambridge.

52. White-ground lekythos: Ht. 39 cm., by the Woman Painter, ca. 425 B.C., Athens NM 1956.
   Photo: Hirmer Fotoarchiv München.

53. White-ground lekythos: Ht. 48 cm., attributed to Group R, ca. 425–400 B.C., Athens NM 1816.
   Photo: Hirmer Fotoarchiv München.

54. Rf stamnos: Ht. 44 cm., by the Kleophon Painter, ca. 430 B.C., Munich 2415.
   Photo: Hirmer Fotoarchiv München.

55. Rf dinos: Ht. 24.5 cm., by the Dinos Painter, ca. 430–420 B.C., Berlin F 2402.
   Photo: Staatliche Museen, Berlin.

56. Rf kalpis: Ht. 52.1 cm., by the Meidias Painter, ca. 410 B.C., London E 224.
   Photo: The British Museum, London.

57. Rf neck-amphora: Ht. 34.9 cm., by the Suessula Painter, ca. 400–375 B.C., New York 17.46.1.
    Photo: The Metropolitan Museum of Art, New York.

58. Rf volute-krater: Ht. 75 cm., by the Pronomos Painter, end of fifth or early fourth century B.C., Naples 3240.
    Photo: Hirmer Fotoarchiv München.

59. Rf kalpis: Ht. 43.6 cm., by the Meleager Painter, early fourth century B.C., New York 56.171.56.
    Photo: The Metropolitan Museum of Art, New York.

60. Rf volute-krater: Size of fragments: 21.6 x 17.2 cm. and 14.6 x 10.2 cm., by the Painter of the New York Centauromachy, ca. 400 B.C., New York 06.1021.140 a.b.
    Photo: The Metropolitan Museum of Art, New York.

61. Rf kalpis: Ht. 44.8 cm., by the Erbach Painter, early fourth century B.C., New York 56.171.55.
    Photo: The Metropolitan Museum of Art, New York.

62. Rf kalpis: Ht. 29.2 cm., unattributed, ca. 370–350 B.C., New York 06.1021.184.
    Photo: The Metropolitan Museum of Art, New York.

63. Rf chous: Ht. 23.5 cm., by the Pompe Painter, mid-fourth century B.C., New York, N.Y. 25.190.
    Photo: The Metropolitan Museum of Art, New York.

64. Rf pelike: Ht. 42.5 cm., by the Marsyas Painter, ca. 350–325 B.C., London 62.5-30 (E 424).
    Photo: The British Museum, London.

FIGURES IN TEXT

1. Type A Amphora
2. Type B Amphora
3. Type C Amphora
4. Type A Neck-amphora
5. Type B Neck-amphora
6. Type D Neck-amphora
7. Pelike
8. Stamnos
9. Loutrophoros
10. Neck-hydria
11. Kalpis
12. Volute-krater
13. Column-krater
14. Calyx-krater
15. Bell-krater
16. Shoulder lekythos
17. Squat lekythos
18. Type A Kylix
19. Type B Kylix
20. Type C Kylix
21. Stemless Kylix
22. Skyphos

PREFACE

In my *Handbook of Greek Pottery*,[1] I sought to introduce ancient Greek pottery of the period 1050–320 B.C. to the amateur. In a companion to the present volume, I attempted to expand on one segment of this field, the black-figure technique, which was employed in Athens from the end of the seventh century to the mid-fifth century B.C.[2]

The present book continues the story, picking up with the invention of the red-figure technique about 530 B.C. and following through to the decline of Greek painted pottery in the latter part of the fourth century B.C. It is somewhat longer than my black-figure guide, since red-figure is better known. Red-figure was produced over a somewhat longer period of time. More of it seems to have been found—or at least identified. It seems also to have been more thoroughly studied. Thus, Sir John Davidson Beazley catalogued black-figure in one volume, but took three volumes to cover red-figured vases.

My purpose in presenting these books has not been to explore new areas nor to present new facts. Instead, it has been to provide in three compact volumes information gathered from diverse sources. Some of these sources are scholarly works long out of print; others are very expensive; many are rarely available to the neophyte. In other words, it has been my hope to make it easier for both the amateur and the beginning student to appreciate ancient Greek pottery.

I have been relatively sparing in the use of notes since, in a secondary work, I consider them rather pedantic and often tedious to the reader. I have generally employed them only to amplify some point in the text. I hope that the scholars whose works I have used will accept my broad but most sincere expressions of indebtedness.

1. Robert S. Folsom, *Handbook of Greek Pottery: A Guide for Amateurs* (London: Faber and Faber Ltd., 1967).
2. _____,*Attic Black-Figured Pottery* (Park Ridge, N.J.: Noyes Press, 1975), hereafter cited as *Attic B-f Pottery*.

The first two chapters of this book deal primarily with background material. Thus, the introductory chapter contains a quick summary of the red-figure technique, elucidates such subjects as dating of pottery, inscriptions found, and the production of colors, defines various terms used in subsequent chapters and sets forth my concept of the art of vase painting. The second chapter discusses the vase shapes employed in the red-figure technique, tracing their origin, rise and decline in popularity, with emphasis on the major shapes, and concludes with a brief section devoted to the more prominent potters. The following five chapters trace stylistic developments in general terms, discussing the contributions of the major artists of each period. Chapter VI, dealing with the white-ground technique, constitutes a slight deviation from the general theme of the red-figure story. Appendix II is designed to supplement discussion of stylistic developments by means of drawings. Other appendices support or supplement the text.

Arlington, Va.   *Robert S. Folsom*
July, 1976

ACKNOWLEDGMENTS

My greatest debt is to the late Sir John Davidson Beazley, especially for his comprehensive and authoritative listing of painters and their works, entitled *Attic Red-Figure Vase Painters*.* The organization of Chapters III through VII devoted to the more important painters generally follows the organization of Beazley's three volume classic. Similarly, Appendix III listing potters and Appendix IV listing *kalos* and *kalé* names as well as much of the commentary on painters' associations and styles, are directly from Beazley's *Attic Red-figure Vase Painters* (cited as *ARV* in the text) as amended by his *Paralipomena*.

To Joseph Veach Noble I owe a very special debt, not merely for the information contained in his book *The Techniques of Painted Attic Pottery*, but also for his assistance with the section in my introduction dealing with colors.

To the late Miss Gisela M.A. Richter also must go a major share of credit for the commentary on the associations between various painters and their distinctive characteristics as well as for Appendix II dealing with stylistic characteristics of the development of the red-figure technique. I owe an immense debt to her for her *Attic Red-figured Vases* as a primary source.

Arias and Hirmer's *A History of Greek Vase Painting*, translated and revised by B.B. Shefton, also has been a source of information about potters, painters and their styles as well as being most useful in its beautiful display of illustrations, from which I have made most of the line drawings shown in Appendix II.

R.M. Cook's *Greek Painted Pottery*, similarly, was invaluable in its commentary on stylistic developments.

The chapter on white-ground vase painting would have been impossible had it not been for Beazley's *Attic White Lekythoi*.

For my chapter on the shapes of vases, I am indebted particularly to Miss Gisela M.A. Richter and to Miss Marjorie J. Milne for their *Shapes and Names of Athenian Vases* as well as to R.M. Cook for his sketches and descriptions in *Greek Painted Pottery*.

*See bibliography for complete citations of authors and works.

xv

Other authors whose works I have employed in writing this book, and on whom I have drawn liberally, especially for commentary on painters' styles, are listed in the bibliography and to each I express my gratitude.

While giving complete acknowledgment of my debt to the various scholars whose works I have used, I accept full responsibility for any errors derived from my reading or interpretation of their words. I accept also full responsibility for my own views and observations.

Among individuals who have been of personal assistance to me, I wish to thank Miss Yvonne Diaz, Mrs. A. Allen King, Mrs. Fernande Fanfant, Miss Alice Wade and Mr. William B. Folsom who typed portions of my manuscript. Mrs. Jane Biers has been of special help in looking up details for me, and Mr. Lewis C. Mattison has been of great assistance in making editorial suggestions.

To the following I am indebted for their courtesy and time in permitting me behind the scenes in various museums or for their advice: Dr. Eugene Vanderpool (American School of Classical Studies and the Agora Museum, Athens), Professor David Mitten (Fogg Museum, Harvard University, Boston), Miss Anna Booth (Rhode Island School of Design, Providence, R.I.), Dr. Cornelius Vermeule and Dr. Emily Vermeule (Boston Museum of Fine Arts, Boston, Mass.), Miss Barbara Rumpf (Seattle, Washington), Dr. Henry P. Maynard (Wadsworth Atheneum, Hartford, Conn.), Mr. E.R. Gallagher (Registrar of the Palace of the Legion of Honor, San Francisco, California), Dr. Photis Petsas (then Ephor of Antiquities in Thessaloniki) and Dr. Vassos Karageorghis (Director of the Cyprus Archaeological Service).

Finally, I owe appreciation to my wife, Florence, for helpful suggestions, proof-reading and, generally, for putting up with me during the years this book was in preparation.

I

Introduction

SUMMARY OF THE RED-FIGURE TECHNIQUE

A summary of the background and development of the red-figure technique of vase painting appears useful to set the stage for subsequent more detailed examination.

During the seventy or eighty years prior to ca. 530 B.C., Attic vase painters had decorated their products with black silhouettes on an orange-red background. The *black-figure technique* with a light background had been employed first in Corinth for an *Animal style* and, later, in Athens with an orange-red background for a *Human style*. Relatively liberal use of red, purple and white, in addition to the black of the figures and the orange-red of the background, characterized the technique along with much use of fine incision for details. Attic black-figure was brought to its apogee by the master painters Lydos, the Amasis Painter and above all by Exekias in the years ca. 550 to 520 B.C.

About 530 B.C., a new way of painting, the *red-figure technique*, was invented in Attica, possibly by the Andokides Painter. This constituted a major change from the old black-figure technique. It involved "reserving" the figures in orange-red against a black background. Interior lines, instead of being incised, were drawn in shades of black. Use of colors was greatly reduced; white for the flesh of females was abandoned (though it was still used for the hair of old men), and the various shades of red and purple were usually confined to inscriptions, branches, wreaths, and fillets.

Development of this technique opened up new possibilities for depicting the human figure. Whereas the old black-figure technique, by reason of its use of silhouette and reliance on incision for interior lines and details, had been stiff and austere, the red-figure technique permitted development of softer lines and less contorted poses.

Of course, changes did not occur all at once. Some fine painters continued to employ the black-figure technique for more than a generation after the development of the new technique—many, however, were minor artists. Some painted in both techniques, occasionally on the same pot. After ca. 500 B.C., however, few good artists painted in the black-figure technique and then exceptionally. After ca. 475 B.C., good red-figure artists worked in black-figure only to produce Panathenaic amphorae. These special pots, given as prizes at the quadrennial games for Athena, were painted in the black-figure technique, and continued in this tradition even after the red-figure technique had become extinct in the late fourth century B.C.

At first the figures in the new technique differed little from those produced in the black-figure technique. Thus, initially, incision continued in use, especially to outline heads, hair, and beards and to show their details; bodies continued to be composites of the parts; drapery was stiff and in precise folds; subjects continued to be drawn from mythology; old pottery shapes continued to be employed.

Soon, however, the old conventions in painting and pot-making gave way. Outlining of head and hair by incision was abandoned in favor of reserving these features against the black background; a hard, wiry, black relief line along with dilute lines and, later, shading, replaced incision for interior details; bodies were rendered in more natural poses; drapery was drawn in flowing lines following the shape and action of the bodies; subjects were taken increasingly from daily life and shown with gestures or attitudes expressive of emotion; new pottery forms were developed to replace the older shapes.

At its best, red-figured pottery was, perhaps, the acme of symmetry, simplicity, and beauty. The utilitarian purpose of each item was never ignored; body, foot, handles, lip, and lid were supplied as needed for each type of pot, yet each of the parts contributed to an harmonious whole. Whether sharply articulated or flowing smoothly from one part to another, the final result was beautifully and simply formed.

The best painting, likewise, was simple. On larger pots, one or a very few characters were posed gracefully with a minimum of subsidiary decoration. On cups, the insides were provided with simple tondos and the outsides with beautifully drawn figures. Painting was not purely decorative nor simply "painting on a pot"; it formed an integral part of the whole, contributing to its articulation or flowing lines.

Extremely careful initial outlining of each figure plus skillful use of hard, sharp relief lines with soft, broader dilute lines in combination, enabled the painters to portray eyes, hair, muscles, tendons, and veins of humans as well as the fall and fold of their clothing with extraordinary realism. The early results were excellent renderings of typical gods or heroes, later, of warriors and athletes and, still later, exquisite portrayals of ideals in human beauty, though drawn with only a few lines.

In the course of time, however, painting became pretty, fussy, ornate, or careless; figures became more and more effeminate and tended to move out of the plane of the pot surface; the emotions expressed tended to degenerate; additional colors were used too much along with applied clay; shapes became slimmer and less graceful. The era of the red-figure technique passed and in the Hellenistic period, pots were plain black, stamped or molded in relief or, if painted at all, very badly done.

Throughout the two hundred years of its existence, red-figure painting was peculiarly human, yet impersonal. It was never purely decorative in the sense of abstract, geometric, or floral design. When shown, landscapes, buildings, trees, animals, in fact, all except the human figures, were subsidiary and accessory features. The males and females depicted, however, were in no sense portraits. They were types—gods, heroes, mythological characters, or humans. The gods, heroes, and mythological beings usually can be identified from the context of the picture even if no inscriptions are found. Trojans, Scythians, Persians, and Greeks of various city states can be distinguished by their dress or armor.

Throughout the Archaic period, emphasis was on action rather than on the individual. Hence, though there was a tendency for scenes of everyday life to replace the world of myth, the style remained impersonal. In the Classical period, there was an ever-increasing trend towards idealization of face and figure, which rendered the style even less personal than in the Archaic period. Later, especially in the fourth century B.C., scenes seem to have been drawn from the commonplace or from idealized concepts of life.

DATING OF POTTERY[1]

Dating of most Greek pottery to calendar years is hazardous. Relative chronology, on the other hand, is much more sure, if one realizes that there were always innovators in advance of most of their fellows, stragglers who continued to work in the techniques of their youth, and conscious archaists or "mannerists" painting in an earlier style.

From about the beginning of the fifth century B.C., however, dating of Attic pottery is fairly precise. Just before 525 B.C., the Siphnian treasure-house was constructed at Delphi; the style of the earliest red-figured work closely resembles the sculpture (especially in lines portraying drapery and muscles) on that treasure-house, thus providing a key.[2]

The visit of the famous Ionian lyric poet, Anakreon, to Athens in the late sixth century B.C., provides approximate dates for vases on which he is mentioned. Pottery found in the burial mound at Marathon and in the debris left after the Persian sacks of Athens must have been produced prior to 490 B.C. and 480/79 B.C., respectively. The founding of the colony of Camarina in 461 B.C., the "purification" of Delos in 426/25 B.C., (when the Athenians removed the contents of graves from that island to the nearby island of Rheneia) as well as the burial of the Lacedaemonians in Athens of 403 B.C., all provide useful dates. The name-piece of the Pronomos Painter may commemorate the visit of that famous musician to Athens about the end of the fifth century B.C. The death of Dexileos, who fell in battle at Corinth in 394 B.C., gives approximate dates for pottery found in his burial plot.

Inscriptions of the names of favorites of the time[3] (*kalos* names) also sometimes provide supporting evidence for the dating of pottery. Thus, praise of Miltiades on a plate, dated to ca. 520–510 B.C., could support this dating, if the Miltiades named as *kalos* is the same person as the victor at Marathon in 490 B.C. The name Leagros, which appears often with *kalos* at the end of the sixth century, may be that of the general killed in battle in 465 B.C., and the appearance, a generation later, of the name

Glaukon, "the son of Leagros," may well be that of the general's son, since the general's father is known to have been named Glaukon and it was frequent practice to name a boy after his paternal grandfather. Many other examples exist which appear to lend substance to stylistic dating.[4]

It is conventional to divide pottery of the red-figure technique into six periods or stages. Each, in its fully developed aspect, has stylistic characteristics which identify items belonging to it. Subjects, for example, chosen by the artists tended to change with the passage of time. Progress was made in the rendering of the human figure and drapery. Styles changed in composition, employment of subsidiary ornamentation and in the use of colors. Preferences shifted as to the types of vessels employed by painters. Such changes once accomplished became characteristic of a new style or period. To attempt to confine these stages within precise time periods is, of course, arbitrary and the transition from one stage to another is often blurred—there are both late followers of the older styles and early experimenters. With this caveat, the stages or styles may be listed as follows:

> Early Archaic Red-Figure Style—ca. 530–500 B.C.
> Late or Ripe Archaic Style—ca. 500–475 B.C.
> Early Classical Free Style—ca. 475–450 B.C.
> Classical Free Style—ca. 450–420 B.C.
> Late Fifth Century Style—ca. 420–390 B.C.
> Fourth Century Painting—ca. 390–320 B.C.

I have used calendar years throughout this book. In doing so, I have employed generally accepted dates, with the understanding that for any date, a leeway of a few years on either side should be allowed.

INSCRIPTIONS[5]

The most common inscriptions on red-figured pottery are those identifying characters shown on the vase. Titles for the scenes are perhaps the most rare. Occasionally, the words of a character depicted are given. Also occasionally, there are such inscriptions as scriptions as a salutation to the user of the vase, a remark about another painter, or a boast. Sometimes, meaningless letters may be strung together. Love names (for boys followed by *kalos* and, less frequently for girls by *kalé*) are found relatively frequently (more than two hundred different names have been found, often repeated many times, with most of them from the period ca. 530 B.C. to 450 B.C.).[6] The most important (but unfortunately relatively rare) inscriptions are signatures of painters and potters.[7] Incidentally, sometimes the potter or painter added his father's name, or the potter and the painter would be the same person and sign as such.

In passing, it may be noted that prior to ca. 490–480 B.C., inscriptions were written in Attic script, but after ca. 480 B.C., Ionic letters began to appear.[8] It is also interesting to note that painters wrote their inscriptions forwards or backwards and at any angle that seemed to them to fit in with the general design of the picture.

Other types of inscriptions, made after firing, appear on the feet of pots and on pot sherds, indicating prices, transactions, votes of ostracism, and the like.[9]

POTTERS AND PAINTERS

Of the hundreds of artists who produced red-figured vases in the years after ca. 530 B.C., very few signed their names. About fifty different names appear with "_____ *mepoiesen*" (_____ made me), indicating the potter, and thirty with "_____ *megrapsen*" or "_____ *megraphe*" (_____ decorated me), indicating the painter.[10]

Thirty different potters' names are found on pottery of the Archaic period. Four others began potting in this period and continued to work into the early Classical period. Only eleven additional potters' names are known from signatures in the seventy-five years after ca. 475 B.C., and from pots of the fourth century only one potter's name is known.[11]

Similarly, most of the painters who signed their works did so in the early Archaic red-figure period. Painters whose names are known from signatures are as follows:

Identified Painters' Signatures

Early Archaic Red-figure Period ca. 530–500 B.C.

Apollodoros	Hermokrates	Paseas	Psiax
Epiktetos	Hypsis	Pasiades	Skythes
Euphronios	Oltos	Pheidippos	Smikros
Euthymides	Paidikos	Phintias	

Late Archaic Period ca. 500–475 B.C.

Douris	Myson
Douris (Triptolemos Painter)	Mys
Epiktetos II (Kleophrades Painter)	Onesimos
Makron	

Early Classical Period ca. 475–450 B.C.

Hermonax	Polygnotos (Lewis Painter)

Classical Period ca. 450–420 B.C.

Aison*	Polygnotos
Polion*	Polygnotos (Nausikaa Painter)

Late Fifth Century ca. 420–390 B.C.

Aristophanes

Euemporos (Mikion Painter—signature may not be genuine)

Fourth Century ca. 390–320 B.C.

(No signature known)

*For reasons of convenience on stylistic grounds I have included these two artists in Chapter VII with late fifth century painters.

Other painters have been identified by their style and have been given names. Such names are based on the potter with whom they worked (e.g., the Andokides Painter), the location of their first identified or most famous work (e.g., the Berlin Painter), a character depicted (e.g., the Pan Painter), the number of a museum item (e.g., the Painter of Acropolis 24), a *kalos* name used (e.g., the Nikoxenos Painter), stylistic characteristics (e.g., the Triglyph Painter), former owners, archaeologists, etc. In addition to the thirty painters who signed their works, Sir John Beazley lists more than six hundred painters who have been identified and given such names.[12] He lists, also, more than 115 "groups" of vases, each group so closely related stylistically as to be probably painted by one hand. Thus, the thirty signatures represent only four per cent of the total of about 750 painters and groups identified. In signing, both painters and potters appear to have been completely inconsistent. Many of the greatest artists never signed their works. Those who did, often signed only a few items and even then sometimes did not sign their best works. [13]

COLORS [14]

Previously, I discussed in some detail the chemical and physical properties of Attic clay and the firing methods employed by the ancient Greeks to produce the *sheen*, the enduring *black*, and the *orange-red* as well as the *subsidiary colors* (white and various reds) employed in the black-figure technique. [15] The methods were the same in the red-figure technique.

In brief, the basic colors—orange-red and black—result from the presence of iron in Attic clay. This enabled it to be fired red in an oxidizing fire and black in a reducing fire. The so-called "paint" consisted of a concentrated solution of the same clay as that of the pot. On the better pots, the entire surface was first covered with a wash composed of yellow ochre (sometimes mixed with a slight amount of the concentrated solution) and then thoroughly burnished. Areas intended to be black were next "painted" with the concentrated solution. The pot was then put through three stages of firing: oxidizing, reducing and re-oxidizing. Since areas covered only by the ochre wash were porous, they changed color from red to black and back to red with each successive stage of firing. Areas painted with the concentrated solution became red during the oxidizing stage and black in the reducing stage, but remained black in the final, re-oxidizing stage. The reason for this was that the silica and illite in the concentrated solution sintered [16] during the reducing stage of firing, engulfing the black iron oxides and sealing them off from the air so that they could not be re-oxidized to red in the final re-oxidizing stage of firing, which was done at a somewhat lower temperature.

The fine sheen resulted from burnishing, plus the presence of minerals with a plate-like structure which tended to align with the surface of the pot during burnishing and sintering.

Most of the subsidiary colors also were produced by application prior to firing. White was made from a pure kaolin clay containing little or no iron. The reds, ranging from purple to deep claret, were produced by various mixtures of a red oxide of iron with water and about ten per cent of the concentrated solution.

Additional colors, also produced during firing, were used in the red-figure technique, especially in its later stages. Pink was made by adding twenty-five per cent of the red mixture to the white slip material. Gray was produced by adding five to twenty-five per cent white to the normal concentrated clay solution. Coral red or "intentional red,"[17] used mainly for zones on kylikes, was made by adding ochre to a concentrated clay solution with a higher than normal sintering point. Since sintering did not take place completely, the mixture returned to red in the third, re-oxidizing, stage of firing, while preserving a shiny surface. It was hard to control in firing, flaked badly, and was soon abandoned.

On white-ground pottery, a dilute solution of the black "paint," which fired to a lustrous golden-brown or golden-yellow, gradually replaced the shiny black for the outlining of figures. Later, in the 660s B.C., this, in turn, was superseded by matte blacks and reds for outline drawing, while solid areas were filled with brownish or purplish reds. Unlike the shiny black and the golden dilutes, the matte colors were not permanent, the matte black, in particular, tending to fade to gray. About mid-fifth century B.C., new colors were added. First were several reds, all of which were relatively fast. Others, including matte ochre yellow, rose-red, vermillion, pink, sky-blue, a matte black, and light purple, were all fugitive colors and were applied after firing of the pot. During the last quarter of the fifth century B.C., extremely fugitive green and mauve were employed for solid areas.

THE "EIGHTH INCH STRIPE" AND RELIEF LINE[18]

In order not to have the black of the background blur into the red of the figures, painters delineated the figures first with a broad band of the concentrated solution—the so-called "eighth inch stripe"—before filling in the background.

Major details were drawn with a fine hard relief line, which presumably was extruded from some type of syringe. Very early red-figure painters made little use of the relief line, but it became the hallmark of later masters of the technique. Some interior lines also were drawn in dilute "paint" with a brush; later, these dilute lines tended to replace the relief line.

THE SIX'S TECHNIQUE[19]

The Six's technique mentioned elsewhere from time to time in the text warrants a few words of explanation. It consisted of painting the picture in white, pink, and red on top of the black glaze (concentrated solution) with which the entire pot had first been painted; sometimes details were added by incision. The pot was then subjected to the usual stages of firing.

COLLABORATION AMONG PAINTERS

Cases of two painters working together to produce a single item are not common, but occur often enough to warrant citation of a few examples. In the early Archaic red-figure period, the Andokides Painter and the Lysippides Painter produced several bilingual vases, Oltos collaborated with the Chelis Painter, and Epiktetos worked with the Euergides Painter. In the second quarter of the fifth century B.C., the Sabouroff Painter combined with the Achilles Painter in the production of at least one item. In the work shop of the Penthesileia Painter, which can be traced from the early Classical period to the end of the fifth century B.C., collaboration of painters was frequent—at least forty such examples exist.[20]

THE ART OF VASE PAINTING

Dietrich von Bothmer says, "What distinguishes Greek vases from all other decorated pottery is that their decoration, both in content and technique, rises above the level of ornamentation and justifies the special term vase painting."[21]

The best Greek pottery embodied a variety of elements. Utility, simplicity, and symmetry of shape combined with beauty of decoration already have been mentioned. In addition, at least three other features of decoration should be stressed. First, the whole composition was carefully designed to emphasize the shape of the pot and to contribute to its symmetry. Secondly, the figures were kept within the plane of the pot surface. In brief, vase painting was not simply "painting on a pot" or decoration on a ceramic shape; it was intended to produce an integrated whole. Thirdly, since their products were designed for use, not simply to be decorative items, the colors employed by painters had to be permanent. This meant they had to withstand firing and subsequent use without flaking, erosion, or changes resulting from contact with water, wine, oil, sunlight or air.

Not all Greek pottery achieved these conditions. Precepts occasionally were ignored (as when, sometimes, figures overlapped the horizontal ridges of a pot). Colors were sometimes badly employed. Thus, white was occasionally painted over black, or reds were applied over white or directly on the orange-red clay with the result that they chipped or wore off in the course of time. Similarly, the coral red or "intentional red," mentioned earlier, was soon found to flake badly and was abandoned. Employment of fugitive colors even further violated the need for permanence of decoration

During the century from about 575 B.C. until about 475 B.C., Attic vase painting was at its best. The black-figure technique reached its full flowering especially in the years ca. 550–525 B.C. and the red-figure technique reached its apogee in the years ca. 525–475 B.C. During these years, the better potters and painters followed the well-established conventions. Thus, though potters developed new forms, they continued to observe the principles of utility, symmetry, and simplicity, whether producing flowing one-piece or sharply articulated shapes. Painters, likewise, employed curving panels, balanced compositions, horizontal lines, and subsidiary decoration, as appropriate, to emphasize the vase shapes. They kept their figures within the plane of the pot surface and confined their use of colors increasingly to the primary orange-red and black.

Exhaustion of the possibilities for further development and competition with the new red-figure technique had led to decline and virtual extinction of the black-figure technique in the seventy-five years after ca. 530 B.C.

In much the same way, once the red-figure technique passed its apogee, about 475 B.C., artists were driven to diverse expedients to find expression for their abilities. Succumbing increasingly to various influences, the art of vase painting began its long, slow decline. Pot shapes gradually lost their purity of line, though for the most part, utility remained a dominating factor for potters. Painters increasingly abandoned the old precepts which had made vase painting a special art. Introduction of the three-quarter facial view, rounding and shading of figures and attempts at perspective meant that decoration no longer was confined to the surface of the pot. Introduction of new colors, aside from breaking with the essentially two-color scheme of the red-figure technique, reduced the utility of the vase as its new colors were subject to wear and furthermore, led eventually to florid, ornate decoration, the antithesis of the old concept of simplicity. Painters who turned to the white-ground technique soon employed highly fugitive colors, which restricted their pots to funerary use and even those were extremely impermanent. Thus, whether decoration was in ornate red-figure or on white-ground, it became "painting on the pot," not vase painting in the ideal sense.

As the reader will quickly appreciate, I have dealt with vase painting as a special art. Others have written from the broader aspect of art in general, and have pointed to developments in the red-figure and white-ground techniques as reflective and illustrative of advances in wall painting and on less durable fabrics, which are now lost. I do not challenge these appraisals. This simply is not my approach. Thus, I regard such developments as evolution from a frontal eye to a true profile eye in a profile face, from a contorted combination of profile and frontal views of the human figure to more natural poses, and simplification of drapery from artificially stiff to natural fall and fold, as advances in the art of vase painting.

On the other hand, I regard some developments as contrary to the best precepts of vase painting. Thus, introduction of depth and perspective (borrowed from sculpture and mural art) seem unfortunate, as they remove the figures from the plane of the pot surface and impair time-honored precepts regarding unity of decoration and shape. Similarly, I consider the use of semi-fugitive and fugitive colors as detracting from the utility of the ceramic product. I admit this is a specialized view, but I regard it as legitimate. My other criticisms, directed against a trend away from simplicity and symmetry and toward ornateness, are, I admit, matters of individual taste, especially in an age when "art" is, to say the least, controversial.

Notes on I—Introduction

1. For more complete discussions of dating, see R. M. Cook, *Greek Painted Pottery* (London: Methuen and Co., Ltd., 1960), pp. 261-75, (hereafter cited as *Greek P. P.*), Joseph Veach Noble, *The Techniques of Attic Painted Pottery* New York: Watson-Guptil Publishers in cooperation with the Metropolitan Museum of Art, 1965), pp. 87-93, (hereafter cited as *Attic P. P.*) and Gisela M. A. Richter, *Attic Red-figured Vases: A Survey* (New Haven: Yale University Press, 1958) rev. ed., pp. 22-23, 141-43 and 156, (hereafter cited as *Survey*).

2. For other cases in which sculpture is believed to have influenced vase painting, see Richter, *Survey*, pp. 43-44, 64, 93, 117, 141 and 155.

3. T. B. L. Webster in his *Potter and Patron in Classical Athens* (London: Methuen and Co., Ltd., 1972), pp. 21-25 and 42-73, (hereafter cited as *Potter and Patron*), suggests that *kalos* names indicate "bespoke" vases (i.e., specially made or ordered) and that a *kalos* name refers to a friend of the potter or painter, to a craftsman, to a purchaser, to a designated recipient of the item or to someone being honored. While this theory of "bespoke" vases may be true in some cases, its general validity appears likely to be challenged.

4. Richter, *Survey*, pp. 43-45, 65, 93 and 117, provides numerous examples.

5. For more detailed discussions of inscriptions see: Richter, *Survey*, pp. 14-21, Cook, *Greek P. P.*, pp. 253-60, Noble, *Attic P. P.*, pp. xii and 68, and Gisela M. A. Richter, *A Handbook of Greek Art* (London: Phaidon Press, 1960) rev. ed., pp. 314-15, (hereafter cited as *Handbook*).

6. See Appendix IV.

7. See below and Appendix III.

8. Richter, *Handbook*, p. 315.

9. See Cook, *Greek P. P.*, 258-60, Richter, *Handbook*, p. 315, and idem., *Survey*, pp. 19-21.

10. There is some controversy among scholars as to the meaning of the word *epoiesen*, some asserting that it means both potting and painting. I have followed the more generally accepted interpretation.

11. See Chapter II, sub-section entitled Potters as well as Appendices III and V. Several potters are difficult to place in any specific period or the signatures are doubtful.

12. Sir John Davidson Beazley, *Attic Red-figure Vase Painters* (Oxford: Clarendon Press, 1963), Vols. I-III, (hereafter cited as *ARV*), as amended by his *Paralipomena: Additions to Attic Black-figure Vase Painters and to Attic Red-figure Vase Painters*, (Oxford: Clarendon Press, 1971), 2nd ed., (hereafter cited as *Paralipomena*).

13. Noble, *Attic P. P.*, p. xii.

14. For this section, I owe a particular debt to Joseph Veach Noble, not only for information contained in his chapters II and III of *Attic P. P.* but also for personal advice.

15. Folsom, *B-f Pottery*, pp. 9-13.

16. Sintering is a transitional stage reached at temperatures ranging from 825°C to 945°C, at which silica, while not melting, forms new crystals or adds to existing crystals, thus, enabling it to engulf foreign particles such as the black iron oxides. Once sintering is complete, the engulfed particles cannot be released until the melting point of silica is reached at 1050°C.

17. Marie Farnsworth and Harriet Wisely, "Fifth Century Intentional Red Glaze," *American Journal of Archaeology*, No. 62, (1958), pp. 165-73, pl. 36 and color plate.

18. Noble, *Attic P. P.*, pp. 51 and 56-58.

19. Ibid., p. 66.

20. See Beazley, *ARV*, p. 877 for a list of examples and p. 878 for a list showing which painters collaborated with which.

21. Dietrich von Bothmer, "Greek Vase Painting," *Bulletin*, Metropolitan Museum of Art, (hereafter cited as *Bulletin*), Fall, 1972.

II

Characteristic Shapes

GENERAL

Initially, red-figure painters employed pottery shapes already in use in the black-figure technique. The spirit of change, however, affected potters as well as painters, and within a few years they were beginning to modify old shapes and to create new forms.

Among new pot forms developed in the years between ca. 530 B.C. and the end of the sixth century were the pelike, stamnos, pointed amphora, and kalpis (or one-piece hydria). With the appearance of these new shapes, the older types of amphorae, neck-amphorae, and neck-hydria gradually were abandoned by red-figure painters.

In the first quarter of the fifth century, two new pot shapes, the Type B neck-amphora, and the smaller so-called Nolan amphora were developed and rapidly became popular.

The old volute-krater and column-krater failed to attract the better red-figure artists and tended to be replaced by new bowl shapes, the calyx-krater, and the bell-krater. Interestingly, mannerists of both the early and the free Classical periods favored column-kraters as did a few other specialists.

One small pot shape, the lekythos, which was to become the major item of black-figure production during the first half of the fifth century, was adopted into the new technique virtually without change. Done both in red-figure and on white-ground, it became one of the most numerous of all painted pottery shapes in the middle and last part of the fifth century.[1]

Cups had long been a favorite shape for both potters and painters and numerous types had been evolved during the sixth century. Never before, however, had they attracted such great artists nor so dominated production as they did in the last quarter of the sixth century and during the first half of the fifth century. At first, the Type A kylix (created about 535 B.C.), usually decorated with a pair of eyes, was the favorite. Development of the Type B kylix in the years after ca. 530 B.C., however, marked the real dominance of the cup form.[2]

During the last half of the fifth century, lekythoi, amphorae, and kraters vied for preeminence, while, in the closing years of the red-figure technique especially, during the first half of the fourth century, kraters, primarily of the bell type, became the most popular shape among identified painters.

Despite all these changes in shapes, the requirements of utility, symmetry, and beauty were still met, especially in the first eight decades of the red-figure technique. During the years after ca. 450 B.C., a mistaken sense of form gradually crept in as shapes became too slim or too elaborate.

IMPORTANT SHAPES[3]

Certain of the pottery shapes employed in the red-figure technique are of sufficient importance to warrant more detailed discussion.

One-piece Amphorae
Three types of one-piece amphorae may be distinguished, differentiated by their feet, lips and handles; all have a neck flowing smoothly into the body in contrast to neck-amphorae.[4]

The *Type A (or Ib)*[5] *amphora* had appeared about 550 B.C. in the black-figure technique and later was taken over by red-figure artists, who continued to use it until about the middle of the fifth century. This type has a flaring lip, a foot in two degrees with the lower part convex, and flat handles with flanges on either side which were decorated with ivy leaves.

Fig. 1. Type A Amphora

The *Type B (or Ia) amphora* is a much older shape, having been introduced into Attic pottery at the end of the seventh century B.C. It has a flaring lip, which is straight to concave in profile, an inverted echinus foot and handles which are cylindrical in cross-section. This form is somewhat less elaborate than the Type A amphora with shorter neck and shoulders and a somewhat more tense belly. The form was popular with red-figure painters just into the third quarter of the fifth century B.C.

Fig. 2. Type B Amphora

The *Type C (or Ic) amphora* had become common during the third quarter of the sixth century in the black-figure technique. Taken over by red-figure painters, it remained popular only until about 470 B.C. In this type, the lip is convex and slightly flaring, the foot is either torus or echinus-shaped and the handles are cylindrical in cross section.

Fig. 3. Type C Amphora

In the early Archaic red-figure period, it was usual practice to decorate one-piece amphorae with panels front and back between the two handles and with the sides of the panels emphasizing the curve of the shape. In the late Archaic period, one or two figures usually were set on a single band of ornaments or stood alone against the black background on both sides of the pot. By the Classical period, one-piece amphorae rarely appeared as painted pottery.

Neck-Amphorae

Neck-amphorae, so-called because the neck is sharply articulated from the body of the pot, had been common in Attic pottery since the Protogeometric period. The tremendous vases of the Geometric period (ranging up to more than five feet or 160 cm. in height) had become somewhat smaller in the Proto-Attic period, and then were greatly reduced in size by Archaic black-figure potters. Several main types may be distinguished.

The *Type A (or IIa) neck-amphora* as taken over from the black-figure technique had an echinus lip and torus foot. Early red-figure versions tended to have triple handles. This type of amphora failed to become popular among red-figure artists and lasted only into the first quarter of the fifth century B.C.

A later and smaller version with a simple foot, the so-called *Nolan amphora*,[6] had a cylindrical handle with a central rib. This sub-type appeared in the first quarter of the fifth century and attained great popularity in the following fifty years, then disappeared in the late fifth century.

The *Type B (or IIb) neck-amphora* was almost exclusively a red-figure shape; it appeared about 500 B.C. and lasted in favor into the late fifth century. This type had an echinus lip (often in two degrees), an elongated body with a ridge at the base and a foot in two degrees (the lower part convex). Handles usually were twisted, otherwise they were cylindrical.

Fig. 4. *Type A Neck-amphora* Nolan Type   Fig. 5. *Type B Neck-amphora*

The *Type C (or IIc) neck-amphora* is the Panathenaic prize amphora shape. Prize amphorae always were painted in the black-figure technique. Occasionally, the shape in various sizes was painted in red-figure, but it never became important in the technique.

The *Type D (or IId) neck-amphora* is usually called the pointed amphora from the shape of its body, which tapered from a broad belly to a narrow base so that it could be set into a stand. Handles on this type usually were cylindrical and there was a ridge at the base of the neck. Appearing late in the sixth century, this form remained in vogue throughout the fifth century.

Decoration on neck-amphorae differed from that on one-piece amphorae. Thus, decoration on the body usually echoed the horizontal juncture of neck and body of the pot and frequently the neck also was so decorated as to further stress the horizontal.

Pelikai

The *pelike* had a broad neck flowing into a body, which continued to swell and sag to a low center of gravity before tapering to a relatively broad base. A red-figure shape, it first appeared at the end of the sixth century, growing in popularity to a peak in the years ca. 475–420 B.C. After a decline in the late fifth century, it reappeared strongly in the fourth century as the only amphora of any importance.

Fig. 6. Type D Neck-amphora   *Fig. 7. Pelike*

Stamnoi

The *stamnos* is a special shape developed during the last quarter of the sixth century. It is characterized by high broad shoulders, a mere collar of a neck and two handles set horizontally (in contrast to the vertical handles of amphorae). It attained its greatest popularity between ca. 500 and 450 B.C., though some painters still favored the form for another thirty years.

Loutrophoroi

The *loutrophoros* was a special type of neck-amphora used at weddings and at funerals of unmarried persons. It had a flaring mouth, a long neck and a tall slender body. Often, when used at a grave, it had no bottom. Occasionally, loutrophoroi were made with three handles, as a form of hydria. Decoration was consonant with intended use (i.e., either wedding scenes or funeral scenes—a few with battle scenes have been interpreted as being intended for the graves of warriors). Loutrophoroi had been inherited from the black-figure technique, but practically none of these vases were painted by the better red-figure artists until after ca. 470 B.C.; within fifty years, they again became rare in well-painted pottery.

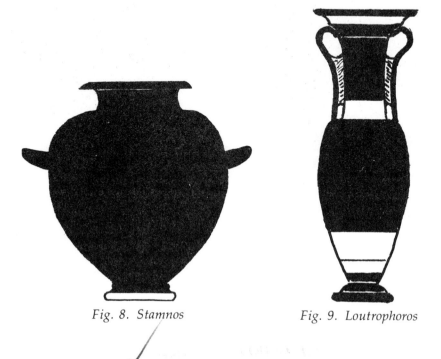

Fig. 8. Stamnos *Fig. 9. Loutrophoros*

Hydriai

Two forms of hydriai, or water jugs may be distinguished, the neck-hydria and the one-piece hydria. Both types had two horizontal handles and one vertical handle.

The Attic *neck-hydria* evolved from a stumpy type borrowed early in the sixth century from Corinth. Given a flatter shoulder in the mid-sixth century, the shape was finally slimmed and sharply articulated by the end of the third quarter of that century after which it became popular with black-figure painters. This type of hydria does not seem to have attracted red-figure painters.

The *kalpis* or one-piece hydria was invented in the last quarter of the sixth century and immediately adopted by red-figure painters. Attaining its greatest popularity from ca. 500 B.C. to the end of the fifth century, it continued to attract artists into the fourth century B.C.

Fig. 10. Neck-hydria   *Fig. 11. Kalpis*

Kraters

Four main types of kraters, or mixing bowls, appear in Attic red-figure.

The *volute-krater*, so-called from its flanged spiral handles, was inherited from the black-figure technique, but never became really popular in red-figure. Examples, however, may be found scattered throughout the period of the technique.

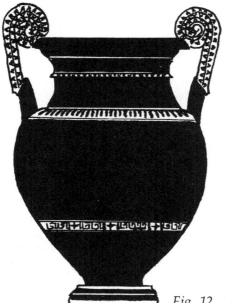

Fig. 12. Volute-krater

The *column-krater* also was taken over from black-figure and enjoyed considerable vogue, especially among the rather poor "mannerists" of the second and third quarters of the fifth century.

Fig. 13. Column-krater

The *calyx-krater* may have been invented in the workshop of
the great black-figure painter and potter, Exekias.[7] It attained its
greatest popularity with red-figure artists in the first three quarters of the fifth century, but lasted well into the fourth century.

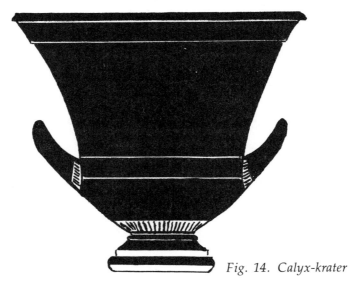

Fig. 14. Calyx-krater

The *bell-krater* is a uniquely red-figure shape. It appeared in
painted form about the beginning of the fifth century,[8] but became most attractive to artists in the latter half of that century. It
was the most common single painted shape in the fourth century.

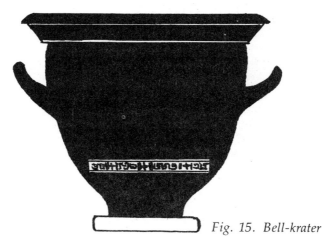

Fig. 15. Bell-krater

Lekythoi

The *lekythos,* originally a small one-handled jug for oil and unguents, was a form of little interest to red-figure painters until the Classical period, when production began to soar. About the same time, the shape, painted on white ground, began to be employed for offerings to the dead, further expanding production of the shape. During the last three quarters of the fifth century, the number of lekythoi rivaled all other forms for first place in popularity.

The most important type of lekythos is the *shoulder lekythos,* a shape inherited from the black-figure technique. It is this shape which was adopted by specialists in white-ground work. Interestingly, some of the larger white-ground lekythoi used for grave offerings had a false bottom consisting of a small cup attached inside at the base of the neck, thus reducing the amount of scented oil required to make it appear filled.[9] The shoulder lekythos appears to have died out suddenly about the end of the fifth century.

Fig. 16. Shoulder lekythos

The *squat lekythos* grew gradually in favor from its invention about 500 B.C., and became relatively common throughout the fifth century.

Fig. 17. *Squat lekythos*

Kylikes and Other Cups

During the Archaic period, red-figured kylikes exceeded in number all other painted pottery forms combined and until mid-fifth century, the kylix remained the most numerous single shape. Even into the fourth century, the form remained one of the major painted items.

Taken over immediately from the black-figure technique was the *Type A kylix*.[10] In this type, lip and bowl form a continuous curve, but the bowl meets the stem at a sharp angle, often emphasized by a ridge at the juncture of the two parts.

Fig. 18. *Type A Kylix*

When (as in most cases) these cups are decorated with a pair of apotropaic eyes on each side, they are known as "eye-cups." This cup version was employed in early red-figure, but became outmoded by 500 B.C.

In the meantime, it had been replaced by the *Type B kylix*[11] in which the lip, bowl, and stem form a continuous curve except that there is a slight step above the disk of the foot to mark the bottom of the stem. Probably the most exquisite shape developed by Attic potters, it is this type of cup which dominated red-figured work, attracting almost all the great masters until mid-fifth century B.C. During the years until about the end of the sixth century, these cups, like Type A cups, were often decorated with a pair of apotropaic eyes and are also called "eye-cups."

Fig. 19. Type B Kylix

Four other cup shapes may be mentioned. The *Type C kylix*[12] has bowl and stem forming a continuous curve, but the lip is offset. It was relatively popular from about 490 to 460 B.C., though never as popular as the Type B kylix. Often it was done in black-figure or simply painted black.

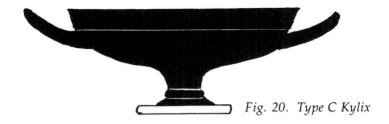

Fig. 20. Type C Kylix

Stemless kylikes, phialai (shallow cups or bowls without handles), and *skyphoi* along with other cup forms appear in small numbers throughout the red-figure technique.

Fig. 21. Stemless Kylix

Fig. 22. Skyphos

REFERENCE TO ILLUSTRATIONS

To aid further in identification of shapes of vases, it appears desirable to cite the numbers of the photographic plates which illustrate the various shapes described in the preceeding pages or mentioned later.

SHAPE	PLATE
One-piece amphorae	
Type A (or Ib)	1, 2, 3, 6, 7, 8, 16
Type B (or Ia)	41
Type C (or Ic)	18
Neck-amphorae	
Nolan (or IIAa)	42
Type B (or IIb)	57
Type C (Panathenaic)	32
Type D (or IId-pointed)	20
Nikosthenic type	13
Pelike	64
Stamnos	39, 40, 54
Loutrophoros	43

SHAPE	PLATE
Hydriai	
Neck-hydria	5
One-piece hydria or kalpis	56, 59, 61, 62
Kraters	
Volute-krater	58
Column-krater	21, 34
Calyx-krater	9, 10, 19
Bell-krater	17, 31, 36
Lekythoi	
Shoulder lekythos	33, 47, 48, 49, 50, 51
Squat lekythos	45
Dinos	55
Oinochoe	44, 63
Psykter	12, 28
Pyxis	46
Kylikes and Cups	
Type A	14
Type B (one-piece)	11
Type C (lip)	25
Skyphos	26, 37
Kantharos	24

POTTERS[13]

There are about fifty potters of red-figured works whose complete signatures have been found.[14] Only fifteen of these signed five or more known red-figured works, while the majority of the rest signed only one known item. It seems strange that they so seldom signed their works; even stranger is the fact that they did not always sign their best works—works which on stylistic grounds can clearly be attributed to them.[15]

Several of the potters' signatures found on red-figured items are also found on black-figured works. Among these are Nikosthenes, Pamphaios, Tleson, Hischylos, Charinos, and Andokides.

Nikosthenes is credited with about 180 black-figured works, 125 of which he signed; about half of his black-figured works were of his special type of neck-amphora designed for the Etruscan market. His nine signed red-figured works include one pyxis and various cup forms.[16]

Pamphaios, who followed the potting style of Nikosthenes, is known to have signed eight cups and two hydriai in black-figure and thirty-six kylikes plus a neck-amphora, a stamnos, and a modified Nikosthenic amphora in red-figure.

Among the other potters working in both techniques, *Hischylos* signed fourteen red-figured kylikes; *Charinos* signed eight miscellaneous items including mugs, oinochoiai, and a head-vase painted in red-figure; *Tleson* signed but one red-figure kylix. *Andokides* signed only six large items and one kylix in red-figure. He was not only a fine craftsman, but also is important because his name has been given to the unknown artist who is generally credited with the invention of the red-figure technique—the Andokides Painter.[17]

Several potters working in the years ca. 530–500 B.C., appear from their signatures to have concentrated on kylikes. *Chelis* thus signed five items, all kylikes; *Evergides* signed twelve kylikes; *Kachyrlion* signed twenty-nine kylikes and one plate; *Paidikos* signed fifteen kylikes and eight alabastra. Incidentally, Kachrylion and *Euxitheos* (a potter whose name is known from five items) appear to have been pioneers in the development of the Type B kylix.[18]

Pistoxenos seems to have had a very long career as a potter, having signed a skyphos painted by Epiktetos prior to 500 B.C. and still being a major potter in the second quarter of the fifth century. In all, he signed seven skyphoi and one kylix.

Among potters working in the first quarter of the fifth century are *Brygos*, with fifteen signed kylikes and *Hieron*, with thirty-nine signed stemmed kylikes and five other signed cup forms.

Euphronios, who was both painter and potter, apparently painted only in the period ca. 515–500 B.C., but seems to have continued as a potter until almost 460 B.C. All of his sixteen items signed as potter are kylikes.

Sotades, a potter working in the second quarter of the fifth century, signed four cup forms, three rhyta and two phialai.

In closing, it is interesting to note that signing of their works by potters was most frequent prior to ca. 500 B.C. and that such signatures kept decreasing until only one potter's signature has been found on red-figured work of the fourth century B.C.

Notes on II—Characteristic Shapes

1. Statements made in this chapter with regard to the popularity of various shapes with red-figure painters are based on the sample of more than 15,000 vases listed by Sir John Davidson Beazley in his *ARV* and *Paralipomena*. These include only items with painted figures clearly attributed to known painters or groups and exclude items which were painted only in black or left unpainted.

2. During the period ca. 530–500 b.c., about 80% of all attributed painted pottery items in the red-figure technique were kylikes. In the following quarter century, some 55% of all attributed items were kylikes and even in the quarter century ca. 475–450 b.c., one-third of all attributed items were of this shape.

3. For this section, I am indebted primarily to Cook, *Greek P. P.*, and to Gisela M. A. Richter and Marjorie J. Milne, *Shapes and Names of Athenian Vases*, (New York: Metropolitan Museum of Art, 1935, hereafter cited as *Shapes*).

4. The one-piece amphora usually is called simply an amphora.

5. Beazley, Cook and others use the designations Type A, B and C while Richter and Milne in *Shapes* employ the designations Type Ia, Ib and Ic for amphorae and the designations Type IIa, IIb, IIc, etc., for neck-amphorae.

6. This sub-type was named for Nola, in southern Italy, where a large number of these neck-amphorae were found. Incidentally, the shape may have been invented in the workshop of the black-figure Edinburgh Painter.

7. Sir John Davidson Beazley, *The Development of Attic Black-figure*, Sather Classical Lectures, Vol. 24, 1951 (Berkeley and Los Angeles: University of California Press; London: Cambridge University Press, 1951) p. 70, (hereafter cited as *Dev.*).

8. The bell-krater shape had existed previously, but probably as common unpainted kitchen-ware. Martin Robertson, *Greek Painting*, (Geneva: Skira, 1959), p. 99.

9. Noble, *Attic P. P.*, p. 24.

10. Richter and Milne, *Shapes*, include the Type A kylix with other cups having lip and bowl in one continuous curve and with the foot offset under the heading Type II kylikes. Beazley, Cook and others refer to this particular type as Type A.

11. Called Type III by Richter and Milne, *Shapes*.

12. Richter and Milne include the Type C kylix with other cups having lip and foot set off from the bowl as Type I.

13. This section is based on Appendix II of Beazley's *ARV* as amended by his *Paralipomena*. See also idem., "Potter and Painter in Ancient Athens," *Proceedings of the British Academy*, Vol. XXX, (London: Geoffrey Cumberlege Amen House, EC 4, 1946, hereafter cited as *Potter and Painter*), and Webster, *Potter and Patron*, especially pp. 1-14 and 41.

14. See Appendix III.

15. Noble, *Attic P. P.*, p. xii.

16. In this and in following cases, the phrase "known works" should be understood.

17. See Dietrich von Bothmer, "Andokides the Potter and the Andokides Painter," *Bulletin*, Metropolitan Museum of Art, New York, February, 1966.

18. P. E. Arias and Max Hirmer, *A History of Greek Vase Painting*, translated and revised by B. B. Shefton, (London: Thames and Hudson, 1962, p. 321, (hereafter cited as *Greek Vase Painting*).

III

Invention, Experimentation and Consolidation: The Early Archaic Masters

EARLY ARCHAIC RED-FIGURE ca. 530–500 B.C.

Invention of the red-figure technique presented vase painters with new problems and new opportunities. An early problem, obviously quickly solved, must have been to provide the outline of their figures with sufficient margin inside so that the reserved red portions did not appear meager when the black background was filled in. Other problems, primarily relating to replacement of contorted silhouette figures by realistic portrayals of the human body and its drapery, posed greater difficulties.

Inherited from the black-figure technique were certain conventions relating to depiction of the human figure. The head normally was drawn in profile and always with a frontal eye; the torso usually was drawn frontally, while legs and feet were in profile. The body was thus a composite of its component parts awkwardly twisted at neck and hips. Men, with rare exceptions, were drawn in black silhouette with rounded incised eyes; in contrast, women normally were painted white and had narrow painted eyes. Incision had been used to mark details such as hair and muscles. Drapery had been portrayed as flat, often with elaborate incised decoration. This had been plausible prior to the 530s B.C., when the heavy peplos had been the fashion in women's clothing and the himation, or cloak, had also been a heavy garment. After the change to the light-weight Ionian chiton during the late 530s B.C., black-figure artists had sought unsucessfully to indicate its folds and fall by the use of incision, while for the himation they used diagonal stripes of black and purple.

The earliest red-figure artists incised the outlines of head and beard and used incision to indicate curls, locks, and strands of hair, but their followers abandoned this practice, drawing head and beard against a border reserved in orange-red. (The difference can be seen even in photographs where incision shows as a very fine line dividing hair or beard from the black background, whereas, when reserved, the division is broader and the tips of hair locks or beard are outlined against a semi-circle of orange-red.) Hair usually was depicted as a black mass with dots or short curls at forehead, temple and back.[1]

The old black-figure distinction between the rounded incised male eye and the elongated painted female eye was eliminated at once, though the eye continued to be shown as a frontal eye in a profile face. At first, the male eye was more rounded than the female eye; soon both were drawn as two shallow curves meeting at each end with a circle and dot or simply a dot to indicate the iris. Gradually, artists drew asymmetrical lines ending in a slight bulge to indicate the tear duct. By ca. 500 B.C., the iris had been moved nearer the nose in a somewhat more realistic position.[2]

The first of the red-figure artists continued to portray the human body as in the black-figure technique, but their successors began to experiment, utilizing painted lines to depict the turn and twist of the body more naturally.[3] To eliminate the incongruity of a frontal torso with profile head and legs, they began to shorten the farther collar bone to show twist of the neck and to angle stomach muscles to indicate torsion between body and legs. Sometimes, one leg was shown frontally to provide greater realism.

Profile views of the human body were seldom satisfactory; in particular, the female form proved difficult—women were shown either with only one breast or with one well above the other. Even frontal views of women were not successful, as then the breasts were drawn in profile pointing in opposite directions.

In back views, a curving spine line was soon developed to show the twist of the body from a full back to profile legs and head; occasionally, one leg was drawn full back to help relieve the unnatural torsion.

In portrayal of drapery, red-figure artists had many advantages over their black-figure competitors in that they could draw flowing lines to depict fall and fold. The earliest red-figure artists took little advantage of this, continuing to draw drapery as relatively flat. Soon however, drapery became artificially elaborate with massive folds indicated by straight or radiating lines and with many zigzags at the lower edge. Later, the central fold was sometimes placed higher than the others and spaces were left between groups of folds; the result was still highly stylized.[4]

As in the black-figure technique, figures were arranged along one line and remained in a two dimensional plane. Depth was not attempted except where figures or their parts overlapped. Foreshortening usually was attempted only with limbs and feet and then only occasionally.

Subjects portrayed in the early Archaic red-figure period were almost entirely mythological, taken especially from the legends of the Olympian gods, the deeds of Herakles and Theseus or the Trojan War, though by the end of the sixth century, everyday life began to appear with scenes of banquets, youths at the palaestra, and the like.

As Professor Cook observes,[5] the red-figure technique in the 520s was experimental, in the 510s new types were being consolidated, and by the last years of the sixth century B.C., artists were beginning to consider problems of oblique views, foreshortening and new subjects.

About seventy-five painters and groups have been identified and listed by Beazley[6] as working in the years ca. 530–500 B.C. in the red-figure technique. Of these, we shall discuss only a few of the more prominent as illustrative of the period.

POT PAINTERS

Originators of the Red-Figure Technique

An artist, now known as the *Andokides Painter,*[7] from the potter, Andokides, with whom he worked, generally is credited with invention of the red-figure technique sometime around the year 530 B.C. The potter Andokides signed four vases by this artist and there is some speculation that potter and painter may be identical; in no case yet found, however, did Andokides sign as painter. The Andokides Painter probably was a student of the master black-figure artist-potter, Exekias, and Andokides, the potter, also probably was his pupil.

Only fifteen works are attributed to the Andokides Painter, all in the red-figure technique. On one of his earlier amphorae (New York 63.11.6, see Plate 1), the rim of the lip has a white background, with Herakles and the Nemean lion painted in black-figure; it is not clear whether he or some other artist did the lip painting. Seven of his earlier or middle period amphorae are painted completely in the red-figure technique. Six of his later amphorae and his one attributed eye-cup are "bilinguals"[8] with the black-figure portions painted by the Lysippides Painter.[9] (See Plates 2 and 3 for a dramatic example of a bilingual amphora.) On an amphora of his middle period (Louvre F 203) he experimented with a white slip for figures of Amazons bathing, though otherwise the vase is painted in the red-figure technique.[10]

Andokides is the only potter's name found on the works of the Andokides Painter. Unlike the Lysippides Painter and others of his time, the Andokides Painter avoided inscriptions to identify his characters as well as the use of *kalos* names.[11]

The very fact that he probably invented the red-figure technique establishes the Andokides Painter as an experimenter. It is evident also in his use of white for the figures on his Louvre amphora, in the white lip with black figures on his New York amphora, and in his willingness to collaborate with the Lysippides Painter in the production of bilingual items.

That he was still tied to the conventions of the old black-figure technique is evident in various respects. He failed to employ the relief line (though it had been invented probably around the middle of the sixth century B.C.) and, as a result, his figures are not sharply outlined nor do they evidence musculature as well as those of some painters who followed him. The male eyes in his early work though painted, retain much of the roundness of the incised male eyes of the black-figure technique; later, he drew eyes with more shallow curves. His male figures have a certain fullness, which makes them stand out, but his women remain in stiff poses with one profile breast and flat drapery, as in the older technique. The drapery of his figures has much rich decoration (complex meanders, crosses, swastikas, stars, and circles) as in black-figure. Similarly, he continued to employ incision to mark heads, hair, and beards. From black-figure, he also took over fairly liberal use of purple for ivy shoots and vines as well as for the flowers and wreaths held by his figures. Black-figure, too, are his base rays, the ivy on the handles of his Type A amphorae, and the palmette-lotus designs and linked pomegranates or net patterns which he used to frame his panels.

He obviously drew inspiration from the sculpture on the Siphnian treasury at Delphi, which was erected just prior to 525 B.C. This may be seen in the similarity between his figures and those of the sculpture, in their proportions, drapery folds, use of three lines to indicate calf muscles, and other details, as well as in his use of the theme of the struggle for the tripod as depicted in the treasury pediment.[12]

During the years of his productivity, ca. 530–515/10 B.C., his style developed from a rather mannered elegance with elaborate details to bold simplicity, especially for his male figures. Throughout, his females remained conservative, stiff, and posed. The satyrs on one of his middle period works (Orvieto, Faina 64) and the Herakles on his later works (e.g. Munich 2310, Louvre F 204 and Boston 99.538) are vividly pictured, strong and limber. His subjects range from the palaestra and chariot races to mythology with Herakles, Apollo, Amazons, Ajax, and Achilles perhaps his favorite characters. His groupings are simple, with large isolated figures providing a fine balance of light and dark. Clearly, he was a first-rate artist, fully qualified to be the innovator of the new technique.

Working also in the years ca. 530–510 B.C., was *Psiax*, another of the first painters in the new red-figure technique, who possibly may be credited with a share in its invention. Formerly, he was known as the "Menon Painter" from the potter of that name, who signed an amphora (Philadelphia 5399) painted by Psiax; his real name is now known from his *egrapsen* signatures on two alabastra (Carlsruhe 242 and Odessa-Zap Od. 17 Pl.2).

Like the Andokides Painter, Psiax was an experimenter. He painted in both black-figure and red-figure techniques, with some twenty-five attributed items in the older technique and thirteen in red-figure (plus possibly three or four other items which may be by him). Two of his amphorae are bilinguals,[13] which are of special interest, since they show the artist in both techniques at the same period of his career. In addition, he experimented with black silhouette on a special coral red,[14] with black silhouette on a white background,[15] and with the Six's technique.[16] Sometimes, he applied clay for spear shafts and he attempted surprisingly bold attitudes for some of his figures. For example, his three-quarter view of one of the warriors on a kylix in New York[17] (note warrior standing at extreme right in Plate 4) appears to be one of the very earliest such attempts.

Unlike the Andokides Painter, Psiax employed inscriptions including, on his red-figured works, the *kalos* names Hippokrates, Karystios, and Smikrion (on his black-figured vases, he used the same names plus Aischis). In addition to Menon, Psiax collaborated with the potters Andokides and Hilinos for his red-figured work.

Whereas the Andokides Painter had been a pupil of the black-figure master, Exekias, Psiax was probably a student of another black-figure master, the Amasis Painter. Incidentally, Psiax, in his black-figured work was very close to the Antimenes Painter, who worked only in the older technique. The two are often called "brothers."[18]

Miss Richter[19] described Psiax' style concisely as characterized by "dainty grace and meticulous execution, with a delicate, slightly hesitant line and . . . wealth of detail . . . distinctive and easily recognized." She notes that similar features often recur, including a slightly wavy arc for the farther edges of chiton sleeves, little circles for buttons, and "small boneless hands with thumbs turned back at the tips." His favorite subjects appear to have been horses and outlandishly dressed archers and cavalrymen (wearing Scythian archers' caps, spotted jackets, and trousers, or Thracian cavalry costumes).

The Transition Painters or The Pioneer Group

Three major artists, Phintias, Euthymides, and Euphronios with their associates and immediate followers have been called the "transition painters" by Miss Richter[20] and the "pioneer group" by Sir John D. Beazley.[21] These painters along with contemporary cup painters (discussed later) set the course of the new technique by introducing a more ample style of drawing, by discarding many of the old black-figure conventions employed by their predecessors, and by addressing themselves to the problems posed with regard to realistic portrayal of the human figure and its drapery.

Phintias is believed by some to have been a pupil of Psiax; if so, he improved upon his teacher. Painting in the years from about 520 b.c. until about 500 b.c., he helped to establish a monumental style on large vases of which he has eleven attributed items along with six kylikes. Though his figures are massive, they are graceful and appear to move lightly. Apparently he never became as interested in anatomical details as some of his contemporaries, since even in his later works, his drawing of muscles and his attempts at foreshortening appear academic rather than based on personal observation. Typical works by Phintias are a hydria (London E 159; see Plate 5) showing youths at a fountain and a Type A amphora (Louvre G 42; see Plate 6) depicting Tityos and Leto.

Still influenced by older conventions, Phintias employed much purple, used black-figure base rays, often used black-figure designs on the side borders of his panels, and employed incision to outline hair and locks. On the other hand, he frequently placed red-figure border designs above and below his panels and sometimes reserved locks of hair. He drew eyes with asymmetrical curves and with a small bulge to indicate the tear duct; often his eyes have elaborate eyelashes. Like others of his time, he was careful in showing intricate folds of drapery.

His earliest attributed item is a kylix (Munich 2590), signed by the potter Deiniades, the only potter with whom he is known to have worked. Phintias may also have been a potter, since the name appears with *epoieson* on two araballoi[22] without figure painting and on at least one cup which was painted by another artist.[23] As painter, he signed six works.[24] Incidentally, he was careless in writing his name, spelling it variously as Phintias, Philtias, Phintis and Phitias.

He made much use of inscriptions to identify his characters and to name favorites of the period. His *kalos* names include Chairias, Megakles, Sostratos, Tlempolemos, and Leagros certainly, Philon and Smikythos (both without *kalos*) and, perhaps, also Epilykos.[25] In a rather unusual inscription, he wrote "this is for you beautiful Euthymides" on one of his hydriai (Munich 2421), referring in this case to one of the other great vase painters of the period.

He seems to have preferred picturing banqueting and athletics, but also depicted such mythological scenes as the Trojan war and the adventures of Theseus and Herakles.

The signature of *Euthymides* has been found with the words *egrapsen* or *egraphe* on six works,[26] in at least three cases with *son of Pollias* added.[27] Working in the last decade or decade and a half of the sixth century, he is one of the great and original masters of the early Archaic style. Twenty-one items are attributed to Euthymides, most of them large pots on which he painted in a monumental style.

His humans are heavier than those of Phintias, and like them, still more or less pieced together, however, Euthymides' lines are drawn with complete assurance. Beautifully posed in better compositions than those of Phintias; they have greater roundness, and his use of both black and golden-brown dilute lines shows greater interest in anatomy than Phintias had shown.

The revelers on one of his amphorae (Munich 2307; see Plate 7) are by far the most successful examples of three-quarter front and back views of the human figure drawn by any artist prior to the end of the sixth century. In this respect, his challenge on the same amphora "as never Euphronios," in reference to a great rival, is valid, though in other respects Euphronios was his superior.

In addition to this unique boast, Euthymides employed inscriptions to identify his characters and to name favorites of the time; among his *kalos* inscriptions are the names Leagros and Megakles plus, possibly, Damas and Smikythos (i.e., without *kalos*). No potters' names are associated with Euthymides, though on a kylix in Florence apparently there was once such a signature, which is now lost. At least once, on his best work, another amphora in Munich (2309; see Plate 8), he included the words of characters shown.

Despite his originality, like others of his time, he continued to use palmette, lotus, pomegranate, and other black-figure subsidiary designs to frame the sides and bases of his panels (with red-figure border designs above) and to use black-figure base rays. He employed incision in combination with reserving to outline hair and beard and drew eyes with asymmetrical curves showing the tear duct. Interested in anatomical detail, he experimented with a variety of poses for his male figures providing detailed rendering of chest and abdominal muscles. His female figures were not as stiff and posed as those of his predecessors, moving freely and lightly; however, despite his versatility in rendering the male figure, his profile females had only one breast. His rich drapery was drawn with ease and assurance, showing wide flat areas between groups of pleats.

His favorite scenes showed athletes, the arming and departure of warriors, and banqueting revels. Less interested in mythology than in everyday life, his subjects nevertheless included

Theseus, Korone, Helen, Apollo, Leto, and Hektor.

Euphronios, like Phintias and Euthymides, was primarily a painter of monumental scenes on large pots. Painting in the last ten or fifteen years of the sixth century, he is clearly one of the great masters of the epoch, rivaled only by Euthymides as a pot painter. Even on small items, his work ranks with the best of the period; thus, his aristocratic youth on horseback on the inside of a kylix (Munich 2620), painted in coral red, stands with the best work of the cup specialists of these years. Among his followers are some of the best cup painters of the late Archaic period.

His name appears on six items with *egrapsen*,[28] thus as painter, and on ten as potter, with the word *epoiesen*. On two items his name appears without a verb; one probably was signed as painter, the other as potter. An additional item had a signature which is now missing. Though there are several other possibilities,[29] it appears that Euphronios worked as a painter in the period ca. 515–500 B.C. and as a potter in the following years until about 460 B.C. In no case found as yet, did he sign as both potter and painter on the same vase. The potters with whom he is known to have worked as a painter are Euxitheos and Kachrylion.

A total of twenty-five red-figured works are attributed to Euphronios as a painter, most of them large items such as kraters and amphorae, but he decorated other items including five kylikes. He also painted at least one black-figured item, a Panathenaic amphora, which may have been a prize at the Athenian games.

A master of design and an artist of great power and originality, he painted with sure precision and fluent command of line. He depicted his large figures at rest or in strained attitudes with a wealth of anatomical detail using the fine black relief line, golden-brown dilute lines, dilute shading and evidencing close observation of the male body. He understood pain and could portray it, as on his calyx-krater (Louvre G 103; see Plate 9) which shows the giant Antaios in the grip of Herakles, baring his teeth and rolling his eyes upward in anguish. Similarly he could portray pathos, as is shown on his newly-discovered calyx-krater (New York 1972.11.10; see Plate 10) depicting Sleep and Death removing the body of Sarpedon from the battle field at Troy.[30]

Despite his detailed depiction of muscles, tendons, joints, and even fingernails, he did not allow detail to dominate his work.

Sometimes, however, he tended to overcrowd his scenes and sometimes he allowed his interest in anatomy to betray him into affected or awkward poses. Like others of his time, he showed women either with one breast or with two pointing in opposite directions. However, he was excellent in the portrayal of the fall and fold of drapery in the style of the period. Over-all, he achieved success in conveying strength and an air of grandeur in his scenes of the palaestra, banqueting and the adventures of Herakles.

Euphronios was fairly liberal in the use of inscriptions to identify the participants in his pictures and employed the *kalos* names Antias, Leagros, Melas, Philiades, Smikythos, and Xenon and perhaps Lykos, although this appears more likely to be the name of an athlete depicted.

He is responsible for breaking even further than most of his contemporaries from the black-figure technique. Thus, except for black-figure base rays and occasional meanders or ivy, most of his subsidiary designs are in red-figure. Though he used incision to outline hair on some of his earlier works, he later turned to reserving—on one of his earliest works he even drew the hair and beard of Antaios against a dilute background.

There were, of course, other excellent pot painters during these years among whom may be mentioned *Smikros* a follower and imitator of Euphronios, whose scenes have life and realism. There were also followers of Euthymides, including the *Sosias Painter,* who ranks almost with his master, the *Painter of Acropolis 24, Hypsis,* the *Dikaios Painter* and the *Gales Painter.* To discuss them, however, would add detail, but little of substance to the story of the development of the red-figure technique.

CUP PAINTERS

Oltos, whose name is known from *egrapsen* signatures on two kylikes (Berlin 2264 and Tarquinia RC 6848; see below) is among the first of the great red-figure cup painters. He appears to have had a long career lasting from ca. 525 to 500 B.C. He is credited with 140 kylikes among his total of some 157 attributed works. He decorated his early kylikes with apotropaic eyes on one or both sides and often painted the interiors of these eye-cups in black-figure, while doing the outsides in red-figure.[31] In his middle and late years, he decorated his kylikes almost entirely in red-figure.[32] Some of these are decorated only on the inside and many of his later cups are rather rough. Other shapes that he painted include small items such as skyphoi and plates and large items such as amphorae and pskyters. Incidentally, some of his best work is to be found on these larger shapes. Among his better works are a Type B kylix, a pskyter and a Nikosthenic type amphora. The kylix (Tarquinia RC 6848; see Plate 11) is signed by Oltos as painter and by Euxitheos as potter and depicts various deities. The pskyter (New York 10.210.18; see Plate 12) shows athletes working with their trainers. The Nikosthenic type neck-amphora (Louvre G 2; see Plate 13) is signed by the potter Pamphaios, and pictures a satyr and a maenad.

The affected hand gestures and drapery portrayed in his early work are close to those of the Andokides Painter, who probably was his teacher. Later, apparently, he was influenced by Euphronios in his choice of lively scenes, though he never developed the latter's interest in detailed portrayal of anatomy. In contrast, he was economical in use of line, almost sketchy, concentrating on strongly outlined figures, which, in consequence, appear sturdy, thick-set and simple. As Miss Richter states, each figure "stands out as a separate design, skillfully adjusted to the curving space."[33]

It has been said that there is much repetition in Oltos' work, with the same figures often recurring. While this may be true as regards the drawing of the figures, it should not be taken to mean that his work lacks originality or that it is monotonous. He almost never duplicated a scene, giving his characters new companions, new identities and placing them in new situations. Except on his black-figured kylix interiors, he seems to have abandoned incision, reserving hair and beard against the black background. He too had trouble with the female form, but mastered the male figure, even experimenting with foreshortening by angling stomach muscles to suggest torsion. He was excellent at portrayal of drapery with a few simple lines.

Though fully competent in the black-figure technique, as evidenced by the interiors of his bilingual cups, Oltos was almost wholly free of its influence in his red-figured work. On some of his larger items, he did employ black-figure base rays, but his subsidiary designs were in red-figure. Unlike his teacher, the Andokides Painter, he immediately employed the relief line, and was sparing in use of the reds, purples and whites of the older technique.

That he was willing to experiment, is evident in his bilingual cups, his attempts at foreshortening and the development of his style through the years. Interestingly, in this respect, he allowed other artists to collaborate with him in the decoration of two eye-cups, Naples 2615 with the Chelis Painter and Palermo V 652 with another as yet unnamed painter.

Oltos worked with at least six potters as is known from their signatures on vases which he decorated. These include Chelis, Euxitheos, Kachrylion, Nikosthenes, Pamphaios and Tleson. On stylistic grounds, it is believed that Hischylos also potted for Oltos. Two more of his kylikes once bore potters' signatures as evidenced by parts of the word *epoiesen*, but the names have been lost.

Oltos employed a number of *kalos* names[34] (Memnon most frequently), as well as other inscriptions such as "I open my mouth wide," "Drink me," and names to identify his characters.

It is difficult to pick out any scenes which can be described as his favorites. He depicted gods, heroes, such as Herakles, Theseus, Achilles and Ajax as well as satyrs and maenads from mythology. Additionally, he included warriors, athletes, revelers, women and animals in scenes of daily life.

Epiktetos is the master cup painter of the early Archaic red-figure style. He apparently began painting about five years after Oltos and, in the years ca. 520–500 B.C., produced at least ninety-four kylikes among his total of 113 attributed works. Like Oltos, many of his early eye-cups are bilinguals.[35] An example is a Type A kylix signed by Epiktetos on the exterior and by the potter Hischylos on the interior (London E 3; see Plates 14 and 15). Most of his other items are plates or small shapes such as skyphoi and kantharoi; among his known works is only one large item, a calyx-krater.[36]

Epiktetos' name is known from forty-one signatures as painter;[37] on one fragmentary plate (Athens Acr. 6) he signed as both painter and potter. Others who potted his works include Andokides, Hischylos, Nikosthenes, Pamphaios, Pistoxenos and Python. Epiktetos' inscriptions, signatures, fairly frequent use of the *kalos* name, Hipparchos, and one use of Chairrippos *kalos* are all skillfully worked into the design of his compositions.

Like Oltos, he was economical in the use of lines. His figures are charmingly simple, graceful, vitally alive with motion, but with few interior lines to show musculature. Clearly, he was interested in outline, of which he had a sure grasp, and in figures in motion, which he depicted with rhythmic simplicity. He was one of the greatest draftsmen of the red-figure technique. As Sir John D. Beazley has said, "you can not draw better, you can only draw differently."[38]

Though his black-figure cup interiors prove his ability in the older technique, he was almost totally unaffected by it in his red-figured work. In addition to his normal red-figure and occasional black-figure painting, he employed coral red at least once.[39] He collaborated in the decoration of two kylikes, in one case, with the Euergides Painter and, in the other, with an unnamed painter close to the Euergides Painter.[40]

Epiktetos' mythological scenes appear to be restricted more or less to the deeds of Herakles, Achilles and Theseus plus Dionysian revels with satyrs and maenads. His depictions of everyday life, however, are numerous and varied with warriors, fights, youths, athletes, women, revels, and animals. The figures shown on the insides of his cups are beautifully adapted to the round space provided.

There were, of course, many other cup painters working in the years prior to the end of the sixth century. Some of these were very competent artists almost rivaling the masters. Among the better painters may be mentioned *Skythes*, whose style is individual and amusing, the *Euergides Painter* with his followers, who painted nimble, vivacious figures with somewhat imprecise flowing lines, *Apollodoros*, a delicate, mannered painter and the *Hermaios Painter*, who was influenced by Oltos. In addition, there were many other painters such as the *Nikosthenes Painter* and the *Pithos Painter*, some of whom were very prolific.

SUMMARY

As we have seen, the last quarter of the sixth century was a period of break from the black-figure technique. In these years, artists of the older technique maintained high standards, not as high as those of the great masters of black-figure, Lydos, the Amasis Painter, and Exekias, but good enough to provide relatively effective competition with the artists of the new technique.

In fact, production of black-figured works even increased over that of previous periods.

These were years of experimentation among the earliest red-figure painters, years in which old black-figure conventions and relics were slowly discarded, sometimes with apparent reluctance. As artists gained familiarity with the new technique, they began to exploit its potential, drawing powerful, strongly muscled figures, but sometimes over-exaggerating poses to demonstrate their new abilities. They obviously were proud of their skill and evidenced it not only in their work, but also in the many signatures of potters and painters. This seems also to have been a period in which a new clientele, the aristocratic youth of Athens, influenced painters to turn gradually away from portrayal of the old myths to scenes in the everyday life of these young men—athletics, arming for war, drinking at evening banquets and revels. *Kalos* (but not *kalé*) inscriptions appear in great numbers in these years. It was a period in which production of cups dominated red-figure production though fine artists worked with pots, especially amphorae and calyx-kraters.

By the end of the sixth century, red-figure artists had made such progress that the new technique attracted all the better artists.

Notes on III—Invention, Experimentation and Consolidation

1. See Appendix II, Figures A1-A7 for developments in the portrayal of head and hair during the years ca. 530–500 B.C.

2. Ibid., Figures A18-A25 for developments in eye depiction.

3. Ibid., Figures A39-A45 for developments in the human body.

4. Ibid., Figures A56-A58 for drapery.

5. Cook, *Greek P. P.*, p. 167.

6. Beazley, *ARV*; see also Appendix V.

7. See von Bothmer, *Bulletin*, 1966, for more details on Andokides the potter and the Andokides Painter.

8. A "bilingual" is an item painted in the red-figure technique on one side and in the black-figure technique on the other (or outside in one technique and inside in the other technique—early red-figure cups thus often had black-figure interiors).

9. In earlier works—Sir John Davidson Beazley, *Attic Red-figure Vase Painters* (Oxford: Clarendon Press, 1942), Arthur Lane, *Greek Pottery* (London: Faber and Faber, 1953), Richter, *Survey*, Cook, *Greek P. P.*, and others published prior to 1963—the Lysippides Painter and the Andokides Painter were regarded as one artist painting in both techniques. Sir John D. Beazley in his *Attic Black-figure Vase Painters*, (Oxford: Clarendon Press, 1956), definitely separated the works of the two artists, regarding the Lysippides Painter as a purely black-figure artist and the Andokides Painter as a purely red-figure painter. He reconfirmed this division in his *ARV*, published in 1963, and in his *Paralipomena*, published in 1971. Arias and Hirmer, *Greek Vase Painting*, and von Bothmer in his article in the *Bulletin*, 1966, also regard the artists as separate personalities.

10. Apparently, he coated the panel with a white slip and then painted around the figures with the usual black on top of the white. See Noble, *Attic P. P.*, footnote p. 62.

11. The Lysippides Painter used the *kalos* names Lysippides and Pordax as well as the *kalé* name Mnesilla.

12. Examples are two of his amphorae, New York 63.11.6 and Berlin 2159. Dietrich von Bothmer in the *Bulletin*, 1966, notes that of more than one hundred and eighty representations of this myth on Attic vases, only one predates the Siphnian sculpture.

13. Madrid 11008 and Munich 2302.

14. A cup in Odessa.

15. An alabastron, Leningrad 381.

16. An alabastron, London 1900.6-11.1.

17. New York 14.146.1.

18. Beazley, *Dev.*, p. 79.

19. Richter, *Survey*, pp. 47-48.

20. Ibid., p. 53.

21. Beazley, *ARV*, Vol. I, Ch. 2.

22. Athens, Acr. Mus. 873 and Eleusis no number.

23. Athens 1628, plus, probably, another cup in a private collection in Switzerland.

24. Amphora (Tarquinia RC 6843), pelike (Louvre C 10784), hydria (London E 159), and three cups (Munich 2590, Marke I and one in Baltimore).

25. This may not be a *kalos* name.

26. Two amphorae (Munich 2307 and Munich 2308), one kalpis (Bonn 70), one psykter (Turin 4123), one fragmentary plate (Adria Bc 64.10) and one kylix fragment (Florence 7B2).

27. Additionally, cylinder fragments (Athens Agora P 4683 and P 4744) with the letters Polio, probably also had Euthymides' full signature. This Pollias may have been the sculptor who signed several bases on the Acropolis.

28. Three calyx-kraters (Louvre G 103, Louvre G 110 and New York 1972.11.10),

one psykter (Leningrad 644) and two kylikes (Munich 2620 and Athens Acr 176).

29. See Richter, *Survey*, p. 54.

30. von Bothmer, *Bulletin*, Fall, 1972. This vase, reportedly bought at a cost of more than $1,000,000, is probably the most highly publicized Greek vase acquired by any museum. That it ranks with the great masterpieces of Archaic red-figure is unquestionable.

31. Of some 44 attributed eye-cups, 24 are bilinguals. His earlier cups seem to have been of Type A and his later cups of Type B.

32. Only one bilingual cup without eyes by Oltos has been found; this belongs to his middle period.

33. Richter, *Survey*, p. 49.

34. Antiphanes, Autoboulos, Automenes, Chilon, Chion, Dioxippos, Memnon, Milon, Molpis, Nikon, Simiades, Smikros, Solon, Stysippos, plus, perhaps, Dorotheos and Smikythos (i.e., without *kalos*).

35. Some 18 of his kylikes are eye-cups of which 11 have black-figure interiors. Like Otos, his early cups are of the Type A variety and his later cups are of the Type B variety.

36. Two of his items are lost, a cup signed by Epiktetos as painter and by Hischylos as potter and a plate signed only by Epiktetos as painter. See Beazley, *ARV*, p. 79.

37. See Beazley, *ARV*, pp. 70-79 and *Paralipomena*, p. 329.

38. John D. Beazley, *Attic Red-figured Vases in American Museums* (Cambridge: Harvard University Press, 1918), p. 18.

39. Two eye-cup fragments (Athens Acr. 62 and Athens Acr. 65) may be from one cup.

40. Louvre G 16 and Naples 2609, respectively.

1. *Rf amphora, Type A: Ht. 57.5 cm., by the Andokides Painter, signed by the potter Andokides on base of obverse. Satyr, maenad and Dionysios, ca. 530–520* B.C. *Courtesy, The Metropolitan Museum of Art, New York, Joseph Pulitzer Bequest, 1963.* See p. 36.

2. "Bilingual" amphora, Type A: Ht. 53.2 cm., Side A in rf by the Andokides Painter, Herakles and the Cretan Bull, ca. 525–515 B.C. Courtesy, The Museum of Fine Arts, Boston, H. L. Pierce Fund. See p. 36.

3. *Side B of the preceding "bilingual" amphora in bf by the Lysippides Painter, same scene. See p. 36.*

4. *Rf kylix: Ht. 11.1 cm., diam. 28.6 cm., by Psiax. Battle scene, ca. 515 B.C. Courtesy, The Metropolitan Museum of Art, New York, Rogers Fund, 1914. See p. 38.*

5. *Rf neck-hydria: Ht. 53.7 cm., signed by Phintias. Youths fetching water at a fountain, ca. 515–510* B.C. *By courtesy of the Trustees of the British Museum, London. See p. 39.*

6. *Rf amphora, Type A: Ht. 65.0 cm. with lid, by Phintias. Tityos and Leto ca.*
510–500 B.C. *Courtesy, Musée du Louvre, Paris. (Hirmer Fotoarchiv Mün-*
chen.) See p. 39.

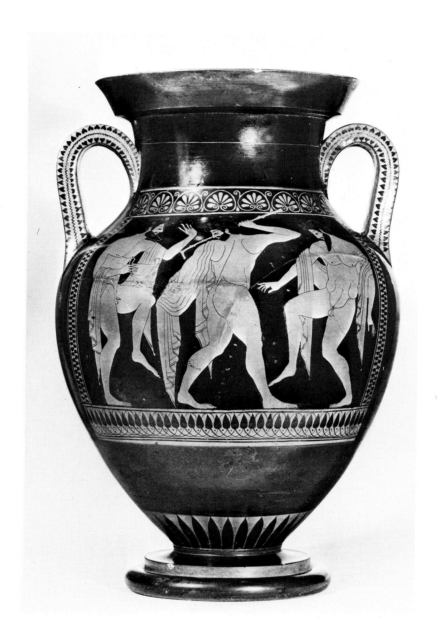

7. *Rf amphora, Type A: Ht. 60.0 cm., by Euthymides. Dancing revelers, inscribed "As never Euphronios," ca. 510–500* B.C. *Courtesy, Museum Antiker Kleinkunst, Munich. (Hirmer Fotoarchiv München.)* *See p. 40.*

8. Rf amphora, Type A: Ht. 57.5 cm., by Euthymides. Theseus and Korone, ca. 510–500 B.C. Courtesy, Museum Antiker Kleinkunst, Munich. (Hirmer Foto-archiv München.) See p. 40.

9. *Rf calyx-krater: Ht. 46.0 cm., by Euphronios. Herakles and Antaios, ca. 510 B.C. Courtesy, Musée du Louvre, Paris. (Hirmer Fotoarchiv München.) See p. 41.*

10. *Rf calyx-krater: Ht. 46.0 cm., signed by Euphronios as painter and by Euxi-theos as potter. Sleep and Death carrying off the body of Sarpedon, ca. 520–510* B.C. *Courtesy, The Metropolitan Museum of Art, New York, Bequest of Joseph H. Durkee, Gift of Darius Ogden Mills and Gift of C. Ruxton Love, by Exchange, 1972.* See p. 41.

11. *Rf kylix, Type B: Ht. 22.5 cm., diam. 52.0 cm., signed by Oltos as painter and by Euxitheos as potter. Various deities, ca. 515–510 B.C. Courtesy, Museo Nazionale, Tarquinia. (Hirmer Fotoarchiv München.) See p. 43.*

12. *Rf psykter: Ht. 34.6 cm., by Oltos. Athletes with trainers, ca. 520–510* B.C.
Courtesy, The Metropolitan Museum of Art, New York, Rogers Fund, 1910.
See p. 43.

13. *Rf Nikosthenic type amphora: Ht. 38.5 cm., attributed to Oltos, signed by the potter Pamphaios. Satyr and maenad, ca. 525–510* B.C. *Courtesy Musée du Louvre, Paris, (Hirmer Fotoarchiv München.)* See p. 43.

14. *Rf kylix, Type A (bilingual eye-cup): Ht. 13.5 cm., diam. 33.0 cm., signed by Epiktetos on exterior. Apotropaic eyes and warrior, ca. 520* B.C. *By courtesy of the Trustees of the British Museum, London. See p. 44.*

15. *Bf interior of preceding kylix: Diam. 33.0 cm., signed on interior by His-chylos as potter. Horseman, ca. 520* B.C. *By courtesy of the Trustees of the British Museum, London.* See p. 44.

16. *Rf amphora, Type A: Ht. 69.0 cm., by the Berlin Painter (his name-piece). Satyr and Hermes, ca. 500–480* B.C. *Courtesy, Ehemals Staatliche Museen, Berlin. (Hirmer Fotoarchiv München.) See p. 115.*

17. *Rf bell-krater: Ht. 33.0 cm., by the Berlin Painter. Ganymede with hoop, ca. 490* B.C. *Courtesy, Musée du Louvre, Paris. (Hirmer Fotoarchiv München.) See p. 116.*

18. *Rf amphora, Type C: Ht. 41.6 cm., by the Berlin Painter. Youth playing a kithara, ca. 490 B.C. Courtesy, The Metropolitan Museum of Art, New York, Fletcher Fund, 1956. See p. 116.*

19. *Rf calyx-krater: Ht. 43.8 cm., by the Kleophrades Painter. Return of Hephaestos to Olympos, ca. 490–480* B.C. *Courtesy, The Fogg Art Museum, Harvard University, Cambridge, Gift—Frederick M. Watkins. See p. 118.*

20. *Rf pointed amphora, Type D. Ht. 56.0 cm., by the Kleophrades Painter.*
Dionysos with satyrs and maenads, ca. 500–490 B.C. Courtesy, Museum Antiker
Kleinkunst, Munich. (Hirmer Fotoarchiv München.) See p. 118.

21. Rf column-krater: Ht. 36.7 cm., by Myson. Battle scene, ca. 490–480 B.C.
Courtesy, The Metropolitan Museum of Art, New York, Fletcher Fund, 1956.
See p. 118.

22. *Rf kylix tondo: Diam. 24.8 cm., by Onesimos, Satyr seated on a pointed amphora, early fifth century* B.C. *Courtesy, The Museum of Fine Arts, Boston, James Fund and Special Contribution. See p. 119.*

23. *Rf kylix tondo: Diam. 24.2 cm., by Onesimos. Slave girl at bath, ca. 480*
B.C. *Courtesy Musées Royaux d'Art et d'Histoire, Brussels. (Hirmer Fotoarchiv*
München.) See p. 119.

24. Rf kantharos: Ht. 24.7 cm., by the Brygos Painter. Zeus pursuing Gany-mede, early fifth century B.C. Courtesy, The Museum of Fine Arts, Boston, Catherine Page Perkins Fund. See p. 120.

25. R-kylix, Type C: Ht. 12.4 cm., diam. 27.4 cm., by the Brygos Painter. Hera pursued by silens, ca. 490–480 B.C. By courtesy of the Trustees of the British Museum, London. See p. 120.

26. *Rf skyphos: Ht. 21.5 cm., signed by Makron as painter and by Hieron as potter. Menelaos and Helen, ca. 490–480 B.C. Courtesy, The Museum of Fine Arts, Boston, Francis Bartlett Donation. See p. 120.*

27. *Rf kylix tondo: Diam. 19.5 cm., by Makron, signed by the potter Hieron. A youth and dancing girl, ca. 490* B.C. *The Metropolitan Museum of Art, New York, Purchased by subscription, 1896. See p. 121.*

28. Rf psykter: Ht. 29.0 cm., by Douris. Satyrs carousing, ca. 480–470 B.C. *By courtesy of the Trustees of the British Museum, London, See p. 122.*

29. *Rf kylix tondo: Diam. 26.5 cm., signed by Douris as painter and by Kalliades as potter. Eos and Memnon, ca. 495–480* B.C. *Courtesy, Musée du Louvre, Paris. (Hirmer Fotoarchiv München.) See p. 122.*

30. *Rf kylix tondo: Diam. 29.9 cm., by Douris. Seated youth and man, ca. 480–470* B.C. *Courtesy, The Metropolitan Museum of Art, New York, Rogers Fund, 1952. See p. 122.*

31. Rf bell-krater: Ht. 37.5 cm., by the Pan Painter (his name-piece). Artemis slaying Akteon, ca. 470 B.C. Courtesy, The Museum of Fine Arts, Boston, James Fund and Special Contribution. See p. 127.

32. Rf neck-amphora, Type C, Panathenaic shape: Ht. 39.5 cm., by the Pan Painter. A kitharist in a long chiton, ca. 460 B.C. Courtesy, The Metropolitan Museum of Art, New York, Rogers Fund, 1920. See p. 128.

33. *Rf lekythos: Ht. 31.4 cm., by the Pan Painter. Eos and a fawn, ca. 470–460* **B.C.** *Courtesy, The Museum of Fine Arts, Boston, Catherine Page Perkins Fund. See p. 128.*

34. *Rf column-krater: Ht. 39.4 cm., by the Pig Painter. Drunken man and youth, ca. 475–450 B.C. Courtesy, The Cleveland Museum of Art, Cleveland, Gift of Mrs. Leonard C. Hanna. See p. 128.*

35. *Rf calyx-krater: Ht. 54.0 cm., by Niobid Painter (his name-piece). The death of Niobe's children, ca. 455–450* B.C. *Courtesy, Musée du Louvre, Paris. (Hirmer Fotoarchiv München.)* See p. 129.

36. *Rf bell-krater: Ht. 36.8 cm., by the Villa Giulia Painter. Apollo, Artemis and Leto, ca. 460–450* B.C. *Courtesy, The Metropolitan Museum of Art, New York, Fletcher Fund, 1924. See p. 130.*

37. *Rf skyphos: Ht. 15.0 cm., by the Pistoxenos Painter, signed by Pistoxenos as potter. Herakles followed by Geropso on the way to school, ca. 470 B.C. Courtesy, Staatliches Museum, Schwerin. (Hirmer Fotoarchiv München.) See pp. 131-32.*

38. *Rf kylix tondo: Diameter 43.0 cm., by the Penthesileia Painter (his name-piece). Achilles slaying the Amazon queen Penthesileia, ca. 455 B.C. Courtesy, Museum Antiker Kleinkunst, Munich. (Hirmer Fotoarchiv München.) See p. 132.*

39. Rf stamnos: Ht. 35.8 cm., signed by Hermonax. An old man and several women, ca. 460 B.C. Courtesy, The Museum of Fine Arts, Boston, H. L. Pierce Fund. See p. 133.

40. *Rf stamnos: Ht. 40.8 cm., by Polygnotos. Herakles and centaur, ca. 440*
B.C. *By courtesy of the Trustees of the British Museum, London. See p. 135.*

41. *Rf amphora, Type B: Ht. 60.0 cm., by the Achilles Painter (his name-piece).*
Achilles on a band of ornament, ca. 445–440 B.C. *Courtesy, Vatican Museum,*
Vatican City. (Hirmer Fotoarchiv München.) See p. 136.

42. Rf neck-amphora, Nolan type: Ht. 33.8 cm., by the Achilles Painter. Eos pursuing Tithonos, ca. 460–450 B.C. Courtesy, The Metropolitan Museum of Art, New York, Rogers Fund, 1912. See p. 136.

43. *Rf loutrophoros: Ht. 92.7 cm., by the Achilles Painter in collaboration with the Sabouroff Painter. Main combat scene by the former and other scenes by the latter, ca. 440* B.C. *Courtesy, The University Museum, University of Pennyslvania, Philadelphia. See p. 137.*

44. *Rf oinochoe: Ht. 33.3 cm., by the Mannheim Painter. Amazon and horse, ca.*
450 B.C. Courtesy, The Metropolitan Museum of Art, New York, Rogers Fund,
1906. See p. 137.

45. *Rf squat lekythos: Ht. 9 cm., by the Eretria Painter. Woman dressing, ca.*
430–420 B.C. *Courtesy, The Metropolitan Museum of Art, New York, Fletcher*
Fund, 1930. See p. 138.

46. *W-g pyxis: Ht. overall 14.3 cm., by the Penthesileia Painter. Judgment of Paris, ca. 465–460* B.C. *Courtesy, The Metropolitan Museum of Art, New York, Rogers Fund, 1907. See p. 144.*

47. W-g shoulder lekythos: Ht. 38.4 cm., by the Achilles Painter. A woman with another (servant?) holding out a stool, ca. 440 B.C. Courtesy, The Museum of Fine Arts, Boston, Francis Bartlett fund. See p. 146.

48. W-g shoulder lekythos: Ht. 39.4 cm., by the Achilles Painter. Seated youth offering fruit to a woman, ca. 440 B.C. Courtesy, The Metropolitan Museum of Art, New York, Rogers Fund, 1907. See p. 146.

49. *W-g shoulder lekythos: Ht. 38.6 cm., probably by the Bosanquet Painter. Mourner at tomb, ca. 440–430* B.C. *Courtesy, The Metropolitan Museum of Art, New York, Rogers Fund, 1923. See p. 147.*

50. *W-g shoulder lekythos: Ht. 48.8 cm., by the Thanatos Painter. Sleep and Death carrying the body of a warrior, ca. 440–435* B.C. *By courtesy of the Trustees of the British Museum, London. See p. 147.*

51. *W-g shoulder lekythos: Ht. 30.1 cm., by the Bird Painter. Youth at tomb, ca. 450–430* B.C. *Courtesy, The Fogg Art Museum, Harvard University, Cambridge, Gift—Hoppin Collection.* See p. 147.

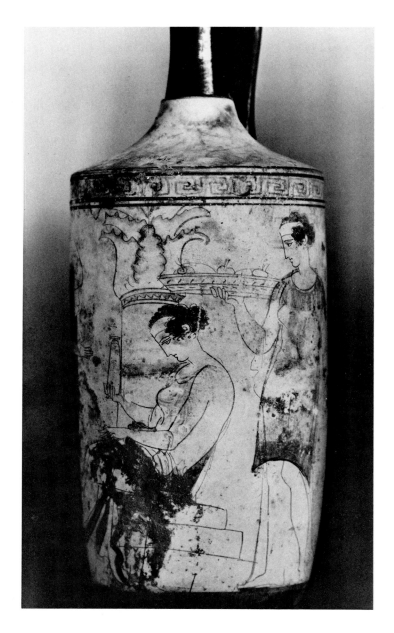

52. *W-g shoulder lekythos: Ht. 39.0 cm., by the Woman Painter. A young woman seated at her tomb, flanked by two female attendants, ca. 425* B.C. *Courtesy, The National Museum, Athens. (Hirmer Fotoarchiv München.)* *See p. 148.*

53. *W-g shoulder lekythos: Ht. of zone, 30.0 cm., attributed to Group R. A young man at his tomb, flanked by two male attendants, ca. 425–400 B.C. Courtesy, The National Museum, Athens. (Hirmer Fotoarchiv München.)* *See p. 148.*

54. *Rf stamnos: Ht. 44.0 cm., by the Kleophon Painter. Warrior saying farewell to his wife, ca. 430* B.C. *Courtesy, Museum Antiker Kleinkunst, Munich. (Hirmer Fotoarchiv München.) See pp. 152-53.*

55. *Rf dinos: Ht. 24.5 cm., by the Dinos Painter (his name-piece). Dionysos with silens and maenads, ca. 430–420* B.C. *Courtesy, Staatliche Museen, East Berlin.* *See p. 153.*

56. *Rf hydria, kalpis type: Ht. 52.1 cm., by the Meidias Painter (his name-piece). Upper zone: rape of the daughters of Leucippus. Lower zone: Herakles in the Garden of the Hesperides, ca.* 410 B.C. *By courtesy of the Trustees of the British Museum, London. See p. 154.*

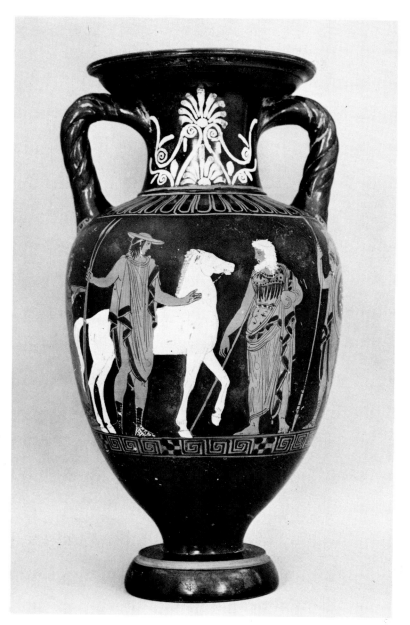

57. *Rf neck-amphora, Type B: Ht. 34.9 cm., by the Suessula Painter. Departure of a warrior, ca. 400–375* B.C. *Courtesy, The Metropolitan Museum of Art, New York, Rogers Fund, 1917. See p. 155.*

58. *Rf volute-krater: Ht. 75.0 cm., by the Pronomos Painter (his name-piece).*
Dionysos and the flute player, Pronomos, with the chorus of a satyr play, end of
fifth or early fourth century B.C. *Courtesy, Museo Nazionale Archeologico,*
Naples. (Hirmer Fotoarchiv München.) *See p. 155.*

59. *Rf hydria, kalpis type: Ht. 43.6 cm., by the Meleager Painter. Poseidon and Amymone with others, early fourth century* B.C. *Courtesy, The Metropolitan Museum of Art, New York Fletcher Fund, 1956. See p. 157.*

60. Rf volute-krater: Dimensions of fragments 21.6 x 17.2 cm. and 14.6 x 10.2 cm., by the Painter of the New York Centauromachy (his name-piece). Battle of Lapiths and Centaurs, ca. 400 B.C. Courtesy, The Metropolitan Museum of Art, New York, Rogers Fund, 1906. See p. 157.

61. *Rf hydria, kalpis type: Ht. 44.8 cm., by the Erbach Painter. Dionysian scene, early fourth century* B.C. *Courtesy, The Metropolitan Museum of Art, Fletcher Fund, 1956. See p. 158.*

62. Rf hydria, kalpis type: Ht. 29.2 cm., unattributed. Poseidon and Amymone, early Kerch Style, ca. 370–350 B.C. *Courtesy, The Metropolitan Museum of Art, Rogers Fund, 1906. See p. 158.*

63. *Rf squat oinochoe or chous: Ht. 23.5 cm., by the Pompe Painter (his name-piece). Dionysos and Pompe, mature Kerch Style, mid-fourth century* B.C. *Courtesy, The Metropolitan Museum of Art, New York, Fletcher Fund, 1925.* *See p. 158.*

64. Rf pelike: Ht. 42.5 cm., by the Marsyas Painter. Pileus taming Thetis, surprised while bathing, late Kerch Style, ca. 350–325 B.C. *By courtesy of the Trustees of the British Museum, London.* *See p. 159.*

IV

Maturity and Refinement:
The Later Archaic Masters

LATE ARCHAIC RED-FIGURE ca. 500–475 B.C.

The first quarter of the fifth century B.C. was the period of the Persian wars, beginning with revolts by the Ionian cities and followed by the incredible Athenian victories over Persian land and sea power at Marathon and Salamis. In these years, Athens was becoming a great city state, secure in its inheritance from the past, proud of its present, and confident of its future. Some of the vigor and exhilaration of these times seems to have been reflected in a full flowering of the art of vase painting.

In addition, by this time, artists were fully at ease in the new technique. They no longer felt it necessary to vaunt their new-found freedom by depictions of complicated poses and over-elaborate drapery. Closer adherence to nature is evident both in the figures protrayed and in the scenes shown. Though there was progress in foreshortening, figures were kept within the two dimensional plane of the vase surface and little attempt was made to give illusion of depth to scenes. Grace of pose, expression of feeling and mood in rhythmic patterns became the objectives, instead of depiction of strength. As Arthur Lane says, "Late Archaic vase painting . . . shows the passion of adolescence, a humanity . . . restless and vital . . . ."[1] Yet despite this exuberance, the importance of the overall design remained a dominant factor. The result was a stylized, but beautifully vital art.

Few new elements of anatomy were introduced. The head remained in profile, with portrayal of a full face most unusual and attempts at a three-quarter face very rare. One minor change was that the chin line (which previously had stopped at the neck line) frequently was extended to show the outline of the jaw. Hair continued to be depicted as a black mass, usually with dots, short curls, or strands at the brow and temple, but long curling locks behind became more frequent than previously. Occasionally, hair was shown as black lines against a light dilute background. Incision was virtually abandoned for marking the outline of the head or strands of hair.[2]

The eye often is a distinguishing feature for work of the late Archaic period. Though still drawn as a frontal eye in a profile face, the large dot (or dot and circle) used to indicate the iris was moved toward the nose, and the asymmetrical curves of the eye were frequently left open, suggesting a profile view.[3]

Relief lines for major details, dilute lines for minor details, and sometimes dilute for shading were employed in combination to produce beautiful portrayals of the human body. The three-quarter view came increasingly into use, with the drawing of one leg full front or full back commonly employed to ease torsion. Even the female form was rendered with ease as profile breasts were shown side by side or in frontal views with one breast often shown in profile and the other frontally.[4]

Though, at first, drapery continued to be drawn in artificially elaborate folds, it soon was depicted less schematically with narrower pleats, no longer in groups, and the lines began to follow the shape of the figure beneath.[5] Zigzags at the bottom gradually were rounded and then replaced by arcs or a curving line.

Mythology continued to provide most of the subjects for vase painting with an even wider range of incidents, though many old subjects were dropped and treatment, in general, was more refined—even satyrs sometimes appeared respectable.[6] Scenes of everyday life became increasingly popular. Thus, fights among warriors and battle scenes decreased in relative frequency, while depictions of symposia, revels, youths at exercise and even in school increased.

In these years, panel compositions on pots were gradually abandoned even on one-piece Type A and Type B amphorae. In place of the panel, artists utilized the whole field, sometimes in decoration going all around the pot (frequent on the kalpis form), or in a type of "spotlight" decoration with one or two figures on each side highlighted in orange-red against the black background.[7]

Composition on cups also underwent change. The palmettes beneath the handles and the eyes, so common on earlier kylikes, were eliminated, while a surround of meander became mandatory to encircle the tondo decoration.

Among pots, the varieties of one-piece amphorae gradually lost favor to neck-amphorae, especially of the small, new Nolan type and the bell-krater was first decorated at this time. Among cups, the Type B kylix clearly became the favorite shape among vase painters of the time.

Beazley lists more than ninety painters and groups working in the years ca. 500–475 B.C.[8] Though this number is greater than that for the preceeding thirty years, the number of artists signing their works is less than half and the number of potters signing is about one-third that of the earlier period. The number of different *kalos* names also decreased; on the other hand, the first *kalé* names appeared on red-figured works.[9]

POT PAINTERS

Two great pot painters stand out as master artists, far above the other late Archaic painters of large vessels. For most of their careers, they were contemporaries. One, the Berlin Painter, appears to have begun to work just prior to the end of the sixth century, while the other, the Kleophrades Painter, probably did not start until the beginning of the fifth century. The former appears to have had a career lasting for some forty years, into the 460s B.C.; the latter's career also was long, running into the 470s B.C. The Berlin Painter seems, once he developed a mature style, to have maintained it, at least until very late in his career, remaining purely Archaic in spirit. The Kleophrades Painter, on the other hand, may be traced through three or four stages and represents more of the later classical spirit than the Berlin Painter.

The *Berlin Painter* derives his name from one of his masterpieces, a Type A amphora (Berlin 2160; see Plate 16) with Hermes, a satyr, and a spotted fawn on one side and on the other a satyr; in both cases, the figures stand simply on a short band of linked spirals. This free field or "spotlight" treatment of showing the orange-red figures against the shiny black background is new and highly effective.

The Berlin Painter has some 284 attributed works, most of them pots such as neck-amphorae (including many of the new Nolan shape and some red-figured Panathenaic shapes), stamnoi, hydriai, and all types of kraters, though he also painted cups[10] and small items such as lekythoi. In addition to his name-piece, he is credited with only three other of these Type A amphorae. Interestingly, he is one of the first to decorate Nolan amphorae[11] and bell-kraters. The latter seems previously to have been a rough kitchen pot.[12] Particularly beautiful examples of his bell-kraters are at Tarquinia (RC 7456) and Paris (Louvre G 175; see below). The former shows Europa and the bull, the latter, Zeus pursuing Ganymede; both are in the "spotlight" treatment with neither frame nor any other subsidiary design except for short bands of meander on which the figures stand. The Berlin Painter also appears to have accepted commissions to paint amphorae for the Panathenaic games, since he has to his credit eight of these black-figured prize neck-amphorae and eight others which may have been prizes.

One potter, Gorgos, is associated with the Berlin Painter and his signature appears only on one of the Berlin Painter's very early kylikes. *Kalos* names also are rare and found only on his early works; they include Alkmeon, Krates, Nikostratos, and Sokrates. Other inscriptions on his works identify the characters shown.

Probably from the school of Phintias and Euthymides, his early work is reminiscent of the latter. Once established, his style was of very even quality until late in his career. He was a master of free field decoration with a few spotlighted figures, which are slender and long limbed, taut and tense even in repose. Drawn with flowing lines, they are finely contoured, strongly modeled and well articulated with detailed musculature. Thus his Ganymede (on Louvre G 175; see Plate 17) is a model example of the archaic ideal in human beauty; like this Ganymede, many of his figures hold large objects in their outstretched hands. His skill in balancing compositions so that the figures are not distorted when seen straight on is evident from a Type C amphora in New York (56.171.38; see Plate 18) showing a youth playing a kithara.

Among his favorite scenes are those showing the gods Dionysos, Zeus, Apollo, Poseidon, and Athena and the heroes Herakles and Achilles; as might be expected, he also shows many scenes of daily life, especially those depicting athletes.

The *Kleophrades Painter*, the other great master decorator of pots in the late Archaic period, derives his name from the potter of one of his relatively early and now fragmentary kylikes in Paris (Cab. Med. 535,699 and other fragments), bearing the words *Kleophrades epoiesen Amas. . .s.* The missing letters, as restored, would make this potter the son of the great black-figure potter, Amasis. Subsequently, one of the painter's late works, a pelike (Berlin 2170) was found bearing the words *Epiktetos egrapsen*, so that his real name is known. It is not generally used, however, to avoid confusion with the great cup painter of the earlier period.

Practically all of his attributed 113 red-figured vases are larger pots such as amphorae, neck-amphorae (including four of Panathenaic shape, one Nolan shape and one of the relatively rare pointed neck-amphorae), various types of kraters, pelikai, psykters, and one loutrophoros. Among his smaller items are included five kylikes, one skyphos, and one lekythos. In addition, like the Berlin Painter, the Kleophrades Painter has been credited with black-figured Panathenaic amphorae including twelve prizes and five others that may have been prizes.

Aside from the signature on the fragmentary kylix mentioned above, no other potter's signature has been found on any works by the Kleophrades Painter. Curiously, he appears to have employed no *kalos* or *kalé* names, though occasionally, he wrote simply *kalos, kalé* or *kalos ei* (you are beautiful) beside one his figures. Otherwise, he seems to have avoided use of inscriptions.

The Kleophrades Painter was a pupil of Euthymides and his first works resemble those of the earlier master in their largeness and strength of drawing. Soon, however, he developed his own highly individualized style. This became characterized by spaciousness of composition, monumental quality and expression of emotion. He liked to draw large figures on large pots, sometimes in rather crowded scenes. His small figures usually were rather summary, but his large figures were drawn with flowing lines and clothed in drapery with delicate folds. Despite much careful detail, its intricacy never detracts from the force of the whole design. Sometimes, his detail is relieved by splashy lines or rather sketchy renderings of hair which seem a bit incongruous.

In his mature work during the 490s and 480s B.C., he imparted to his scenes an air of grandeur and exhilaration that is un matched. Joy, triumph, and pathos are conveyed with convinc ing realism. In the later part of his mature period, he tended to simplify his compositions and drawing with a more dignified re sult; during the 470s B.C., his power declined.

Joy and triumph are evident on one of the largest and finest of his mature works, a calyx-krater at Harvard University (Fogg 1960.236; see Plate 19) depicting the return of Hephaestos to Olympos. The ecstasy of the maenads on his pointed amphora (see Plate 20; Munich 2344) is unsurpassed. The fierceness of bat tle, the anguish of defeat, and the pathos of those caught in the wake of war are all movingly portrayed on a kalpis (Naples 2422) depicting the sack of Troy.

Interestingly, the Kleophrades Painter employed both red- figure and black-figure subsidiary designs; among the black- figure designs are base rays, meanders, and tongues; occasion- ally, he even included figures in the old technique (as on his loutrophoros—Louvre, CA 453).

Among almost fifty other painters of large and small pots of the period, we may mention only a few. The *Nikoxenos Painter* is notable for the fact that his is one of the very few good red-figure artists to paint also in the black-figure technique; he has some thirty-five attributed works in the new technique and about twenty in the old technique. His pupil, the *Eucharides Painter,* also painted in both techniques with 100 red-figured items and forty-four black-figured items (including four Panathenaic prize amphorae and seventeen which may have been prizes).[13] *Myson* was both potter and painter as is known from his signatures. He worked mostly with column-kraters and was the originator of the "mannerist movement" of the Classical period. Typical of his work is the battle scene on a column-krater in the Metropolitan Museum (New York 56.171.45; see Plate 21).

CUP PAINTERS

Among many excellent cup painters of the late archaic period, four master painters stand out: Onesimos, the Brygos Painter, Douris, and Makron.

Onesimos (or the "Panaitios Painter," as he is called in earlier works)[14] may have begun his painting career as early as the closing years of the sixth century; he carried on into the 470s B.C. A kylix in Paris (Louvre G 105) signed *Euphronios epoiesen Onesimos egrapsen* provides us with the painter's name. Euphronios, incidentally, signed several other cups attributed to Onesimos' mature period and is the only potter whose signature is found on any of Onesimos' works.

Onesimos has 161 attributed works, all of which are stemmed kylikes except five (three kyathoi, one stemless kylix and a plate). Among all these works it is difficult to single out items for special comment. A few of his masterpieces include the tondos on four kylikes: a satyr seated on a pointed amphora (Boston 10.179), Theseus, Athena, and Amphitrite (Louvre G 104), Herakles and Eurystheos (London E 44), and a slave girl going to wash (Brussels A 889). Additionally, a kyathos with a youth reading to two others (Berlin 2322) also belongs among his great works.

Onesimos was a master draftsman, employing delicate curving lines even in cases (as on drapery), where his contemporaries employed straight lines; he thus conveyed a sense of movement. His figures are drawn in a great variety of poses and, whether in violent action or in repose, are imbued with vitality. Some of his scenes exhibit robust archaic vigor, others are simple and dignified. Thus the Boston satyr, painted perhaps prior to ca. 500 B.C., is one of his most powerful works, showing strong musculature and archaic virility in excellent foreshortening (see Plate 22).

The Louvre kylix, with its crowded scene and detailed drapery of Theseus, Athena, and Amphitrite, painted during the 490s, contrasts sharply in composition and drawing with the starkness of the earlier Boston satyr. The Brussels tondo, dated at about 480 B.C. is a model of simplicity in both composition and line (see Plate 23).

Among inscriptions, he employed the *kalos* name Panaitios on at least eleven items[15] and he is one of the first to use a *kalé* name (Louda or Lyda). In addition, he employed such phrases as "the boy is beautiful," "the girl is beautiful," or simply *kalé* beside a figure. Sometimes he also identified his figures by name, and at least once he inscribed the words they were saying.[16]

His most frequent scenes take place at the palaestra, banquets, and Dionysian revels; his favorite mythological characters seem to have been Theseus and Herakles.

The *Brygos Painter* derives his name from the potter, Brygos, who signed at least five of the painter's kylikes. He is one of the master decorators of cups, approached in ability perhaps only by Onesimos. He appears to have begun painting early in the fifth century and to have continued for some time after 480 B.C. Of his attributed 243 works, 176 are kylikes; the rest are small items, including lekythoi (at least one in white-ground), rhyta, skyphoi, and kantharoi.

The only potter's name found on his vases is that of Brygos. Other inscriptions include the *kalos* names Alkmeon, Damas, Diphilos, and Philon, the *kalé* name Nikophile, the names of characters depicted and sometimes, such phrases as "the boy is fair."

His early work, during the late 490s and all of the 480s, is characterized by violent action, especially on the outsides of his cups, with scenes of battles, drunken banquets, Dionysian revels, and pursuits. One of these, Zeus pursuing Ganymede, is pictured on a kantharos in Boston (95.36; see Plate 24). He tended to crowd the tondos of his early cups with figures and detail; later, he reduced the number of figures to one or two and simplified the background. In these years, he employed strong lines and drew his figures tense with action, frequently running in one direction with their heads turned looking back at some pursuer. He was, perhaps, at his best in portraying the various moods of drunken roisterers, though he could convey pathos and tenderness with almost equal facility. The heavy cloaks worn by his figures and the overlapping of figures, swords and shields serve to unite his pictures into an even whole.

After about 480 B.C., his work is weaker, the lines too fine, his figures tame and mannered, clothed in stiff and lifeless drapery.

One of the best of his cup exteriors, showing Hera pursued by several sirens, is on a Type C kylix (London E 65, see Plate 25); the signature of Brygos is on the base. Another of his famous works is a Type B kylix (Munich 2645) with Dionysos, a satyr, and ecstatic maenads outside, and with a maenad in white-ground on the interior. Other important works include a Type B kylix (Louvre G 152) with the sack of Troy outside, and a skyphos (Louvre G 156) showing a reveling scene. A typical late work is a lekythos (Boston 13.189) showing a woman working wool.

Makron's name is known from his signature on a skyphos (Boston 13.186; see Plate 26) showing Menelaos reclaiming Helen after the fall of Troy. On this, he signed jointly with the potter:

Hieron epoiesen Makron egraphsen. Part of his signature, *Makr*, with the verb also lost, appears on a fragmentary pyxis (Athens Acr. 560). Hieron, incidentally, signed a total of forty-four known vases, of which thirty-three were decorated by Makron; he is the only potter whose signature has been found on Makron's works. An example is the signed kylix (New York 96.9.191 GR 1120; see Plate 27) showing a youth watching a girl dancing.

Makron has 356 attributed works, of which 345 are stemmed kylikes. His other attributed works include four skyphoi, a stemless kylix, three askoi, one plate, one aryballos, and the pyxis mentioned above.

His style was relatively even throughout his career (ca. 495–480 B.C. or a little after) and is characterized by harmony of composition and delicate but sure lines, which are especially effective in the drawing of the multiple folds of women's drapery. Less violent than some of his contemporaries, his favorite scenes include banquets, youths exercising, Dionysian revels, and so-called "conversation pieces" depicting women, boys, or youths in groups of two or three. In these latter pieces, there is much repetition of figures, but they are differentiated and enlivened by a variety of background objects such as stools, cushions, baskets, and wreaths. Makron also depicted mythological scenes from the Trojan War and the legends of Theseus and Herakles.

Some of his masterpieces include three skyphoi: his name-piece in Boston, one in Paris (Louvre G 146) depicting Briseis, and one showing Triptolemos in a winged chair with Demeter and other deities (London E 140), and a kylix (Berlin 2290) with dancing maenads.

He employed the *kalos* names Akestorides (partial), Antiphanes, Aristagoras (misspelt), Hiketes, Hippodamas, Nikon, Polydemos, and Praxiteles as well as the *kalé* names Aphrodesia, Melitta, Naukleia, and Rhodopis.

Douris, or as he sometimes spelled it, *Doris*, is known from forty-one signatures as painter.[17] That he was also a potter is evident from a kantharos (Brussels A 718), which he signed *Doris egrapsen, Doris ep (oiesen)*, and an aryballos (Athens 15375) which he signed *Doris epoiesen*. The potters Kalliades and Kleophrades also made at least one kylix each for him, while Python, who signed three of Douris' kylikes, is credited on stylistic grounds with most of this painter's cups.[18]

Douris had a long career, lasting from soon after 500 B.C. into the seventies of the fifth century. The number of his attributed works is 284, of which 257 are stemmed kylikes; most of the balance are small items. In addition, three of his known items are now lost and he is credited with one black-figured item, a nuptial lebes.

His style evolved through three rather distinct stages. His work in the early 490s B.C. apparently was influenced by Onesimos and is characterized by animated figures. A discus thrower on a kylix in Boston (00.338) is typical of his early style. During this period, his favorite *kalos* name was Chairestratos, though he also used the name Panaitios. Most of his works fall into his mature period of the late 490s and the 480s. These are conservative, somewhat academic, but expressive, highly accomplished and very uniform in quality. Among his masterpieces of this period are the dancing satyrs on a psykter (London E 768; see Plate 28) and the "pieta" showing the goddess Eos with the body of her slain son, Memnon, on a kylix tondo (Louvre G 115; see Plate 29).

During this period, Douris continued to use the *kalos* name Chairestratos at first, and then added Aristagoras, Diogenes, Hermogenes, Hippodamas, Kallimachos, Leosthenes, Menon, and Pythaios. His late work during the 470s, though lacking some of his earlier vitality, is still strong, as he turned towards the more monumental type of painting characteristic of the early Classical period. Love names on his late works are rare, but include Hiketes and Polyphrasmon. To this late period also belongs a white-ground lekythos of a type later to become very popular. A typical work of this late period shows a seated youth and a man on the interior of his kylix in New York (52.11.4; see Plate 30).

In general, it may be remarked that Douris was extremely able in depicting serene scenes despite the animated nature of the subjects (banquets, Dionysian revels, and the like) and that he often was original in the rendering of mythological subjects.

Among more than twenty-five other cup painters of this period, mention may be made of a few of the better and more prolific. Both the *Antiphon Painter* and the *Colmar Painter* were influenced by Onesimos and produced many fine works. Followers of the Brygos Painter, and also excellent artists, include the *Foundry Painter*, the *Briseis Painter*, the *Dokimasia Painter* and the *Painter of the Paris Gigantomachy.*

SUMMARY

The six main painters discussed in this chapter in part reflect and in part determined the development of the red-figure technique during the first quarter of the fifth century B.C. They reflect the perfection and refinement of the technique after the initial years of invention, experimentation and consolidation. They determined the course of development through their great influence on contemporaries and followers who sought to emulate them. We have seen how they began with either a robustness and vitality or fussy overelaborateness, which they then developed into styles characterized by simplicity, spaciousness and grandeur. Abandonment of panels on large pots and simplification of cup tondos contributed to this trend towards the monumental in vase painting.

With this chapter, we come to the close of one of the most interesting periods in the history of Greek vase painting. The years from about 530 to about 475 B.C. encompassed greater advances in drawing and composition than those made in the periods preceeding or following. During the first quarter of the fifth century B.C., perfection of detail was intelligently subordinated to the essential of the whole to a greater degree than at any time before or after (with the possible exception of some of the masterpieces of the great black-figure artist, Exekias). Without question, the finest work in red-figure was done in the last years of the sixth century and the first quarter of the fifth century B.C.[19]

Notes on IV—Maturity and Refinement

1. Lane, *Greek Pottery*, p. 48.
2. See Appendix II, Figures A8-A11 for developments in rendering of head and hair during the period ca. 500–475 B.C.
3. Ibid., Figures A26-A28 for renderings of the eye.
4. Ibid., Figures A46-A51 for the human body.
5. Ibid., Figures A59-A62 for drapery.
6. Ibid., Figure A46.
7. Neck-amphorae normally were decorated around the pot or with division of scenes provided by subsidiary decoration under the handles.

8. Beazley, *ARV* and *Paralipomena*.

9. See Appendix V for numbers, Chapter I, Section entitled Potters and Painters for signatures of painters and Appendices III and IV for potters' names and *kalos* or *kalé* inscriptions.

10. One of these cups, together with two pelikai, which previously were attributed to the "Vienna Painter," have been shown by the research of Professor Martin Robertson to be very early works of the Berlin Painter, carrying his period of activity back into the late sixth century. See Arias and Hirmer, *Greek Vase Painting*, pp. 343-44, with footnotes to Robertson's articles in archaeological journals.

11. Ibid., p. 343.

12. Robertson, *Greek Painting*, p. 99.

13. The Nikoxenos Painter and the Eucharides Painter are the only artists of the period to work regularly in both techniques, unless the red-figure Bowdoin Painter and the black-figure Athena Painter are identical, as seems likely.

14. In his *ARV*, published in 1963, as revised by his *Paralipomena*, published in 1971, Sir John Davidson Beazley attributed 161 items to Onesimos, thus including most of the works previously attributed to the "Panaitios Painter" (who received his sobriquet from his frequent use of the *kalos* name Panaitios). In this reorganization, several kylikes were assigned to the Eleusis Painter (who is now credited with seven kylikes); others were assigned to the Proto-Panaetian Group (which now has seventeen attributed works, nine of which are very close to the early work of Onesimos). Writers, whose works pre-date 1963, usually separate the "Panaitios Painter" and Onesimos, giving prominence to the former or, sometimes, regarding the latter as a "tired phase" of the former. Incidentally, at one time some of this artist's works were thought to have been done by Euphronios.

15. Other *kalos* names used by Onesimos include: Aristarchos, Athenodotos, Boukolos, Erothemis, Leagros and Lykos (he may also have used Epidromos; if not, it was used by a painter whose work is very similar).

16. Emily Vermeule, "A Love Scene by the 'Panaitios Painter'," *American Journal of Archaeology*, Vol. 71, No. 3, July 1967, p. 313, describing a fragmentary kylix by Onesimos (Boston 65.873—listed in Beazley's *Paralipomena* as 63.873).

17. Beazley, *ARV*, pp. 225-53 and *Paralipomena*, pp. 375 and 524.

18. Arias and Hirmer, *Greek Vase Painting*, pp. 339-40 with footnotes to H. Bloesch, *Formen attischer Schalen*, Berne, 1940, p. 96ff and Beazley, *Potter and Painter*, p. 36.

19. See Richter, *Survey*, p. 59, von Bothmer, *Bulletin*, 1966, p. 201 and Pierre Devambez, *Greek Painting*, (New York: The Viking Press, 1962), pp. 24-25, (hereafter cited as *Gr. Painting*).

V

The Red-Figure Technique in Crisis: Attempted Solutions

EARLY CLASSICAL FREE STYLE ca. 475–450 B.C.

By the beginning of the second quarter of the fifth century, victory over the Persians was complete and the Athenian economy was recovering rapidly from the war. The authority of the old aristocratic families was being replaced by the power of new wealth backed by the poorer classes. As in all such periods of transition, repercussions were felt in the arts.

In the field of vase painting, artists were faced with a dilemma. The red-figure technique had been developed and refined to a high point during the Archaic period. There were few aspects left to be improved. Painters who continued to work in the old style, unless extremely skillful, risked loss of spontaneity. For those who sought new means of expression, the dangers were equally great. Taming the Archaic spirit through depiction of less brutal, less ribald, and less lively scenes courted eventual descent into the vapid. Development of more natural figures and surroundings involved introduction of the third dimension and of colors inappropriate to the technique.

Rapid development of the art of mural painting, at this time, under the leadership of Polygnotos of Thasos and Nikon of Athens, offered new possibilities to artists; some probably moved into that field; others sought to adapt it to vase painting. Again, however, there were hazards. Mural painters could and apparently did attempt the third dimension and could employ a variety of colors which could not be used on fired vases. To the extent that vase painters emulated the muralists, they reduced the relationship between shape and decoration. Abandonment of the two dimensional plane of the pot risked becoming "painting on the pot" instead of creation of an integrated whole. Yet, unless the artists were willing to break entirely with all their concepts of vase painting, only these outlets seem to have been open to the red-figure technique. Some artists, in fact, did experiment with another technique known to us as the white-ground technique, which is discussed in the next chapter.

As might be expected, painters who continued in the red-figure technique tried various avenues. Four main trends emerged: (1) the "mannerists," who clung to Archaic conventions, some developing a new and flowing style with graceful though affected figures, some merely turning out bad copies of Archaic style; (2) those influenced by the muralists, who produced ambitious compositions on large pots with attempts at the third dimension; (3) painters who developed quiet, delicate, less ambitious compositions presaging the classicism of Periclean art, and (4) individualistic miniaturists, who sought to portray naturalism in old familiar scenes. It should be emphasized that the lines between these categories are not always clear-cut. Some artists do not fit them, while others painted in more than one category as they sought to find new outlets for their abilities.

In view of the existence of these diverse lines of development, it is difficult to generalize with regard to all aspects of painting during these years. A few trends, however, are clear; these include an increasing tendency to depict everyday life, a greater effort to express emotion though facial expressions, gestures, or postures, and a gradual evolution towards portrayal of a new uniform concept of human beauty. Where Archaic artists had concentrated on muscles, bones, and the working of the human body, early Classical artists were more interested in achieving graceful, dignified poses, expressive of purpose or feeling. Scenes often were less heroic than previously, dealing frequently with family life. Depictions of battles, deeds of heroes, and other mythological subjects became less popular, with old legends toned down and idealized.

The human body was drawn with a more rounded and sensual look than previously. Foreshortening and the three-quarter view became common, and shading was not unusual.[1] The parts of the body, however, were still somewhat pieced together. The profile head remained the norm, though three-quarter faces were sometimes attempted. Hair was drawn in increasingly varied ways, often as black strands against a dilute background. The Classical profile eye replaced the Archaic frontal eye, though iris and pupil continued to be shown as a circle and dot or simply as a round black dot. The peplos came back into style with its heavy folds and advantage was taken to this to render drapery in less complicated detail and with more careful study of its fall and fold. Though figures continued to be drawn of equal size, they were not always arranged along one line or kept within the plane of the vase surface. Rectangular objects, however, were still depicted in profile and kept in one plane.

Beazley lists about two hundred painters and groups as among those working in the second quarter of the fifth century.[2] Of these, we will consider only a very few representatives of various trends.

Traditionalism: The Mannerists

Though connected with "mannerists" of the early Classical period and sometimes described as their protagonist, the *Pan Painter* "stands apart from them, his quality is incomparably finer; his choice of shapes is not theirs, and it is doubtful if he sat for long in the same workshop as they."[3] Like the mannerists, he tried to carry the Archaic style over into the new period, but unlike them, he was "that rare thing, a backward looking genius"[4] ". . . who knew to a nicety how to put new wine in old bottles."[5] He is generally accepted as the best and the most interesting artist of the period.

He derives his name from one of his masterpieces, a bell-krater (Boston 10.185; see Plate 31) which depicts on one side Pan pursuing a shepherd, and on the other, the death of Actaeon. His 164 attributed works, produced in the years ca. 480–450 B.C., encompass a wide variety of shapes. Among his large works are amphorae and kraters of various types; he also painted many cups and various small items including lekythoi. None of these works have potters' signatures or *kalos* names.

He decorated these shapes with long-limbed, elegant figures, drawn with all the skill of an excellent draftsman and set in scenes of action and drama, often with original or unusual interpretations of old myths. Though he sometimes employed panels to frame his pictures, he made most effective use of the free field, often setting his figures on a line of meander. The figures are graceful, sometimes alert or exalted, at other times quiet in the spirit of the new era. His archaism is most apparent in his depiction of the folds of drapery and in his choice of mythological scenes, but even in these respects he is not always archaizing. His portrayal of the death of Actaeon perhaps best illustrates this. The figures are within the plane of the pot (except for the tips of Artemis' toes). There is no attempt to show depth and the patterned folds of the goddess' robe recall the Archaic; on the other hand, the eyes are in profile and Actaeon's cloak is rendered in the new style. The figures have the strength and clarity of the Archaic, but show a new elegance and convey overtones of feeling that are not Archaic. There is something of the ballet in this scene.

Another of his masterpieces, a pelike (Athens 8693), on the other hand, is powerful in its depiction of Herakles slaying Busiris, King of Egypt; here there is strength and none of the elegance and grace of the Boston krater. A graceful kitharist in a long, flowing chiton on his red-figured neck-amphora of Panathenaic shape (New York 20.245) is typical of his best work (see Plate 32). Two of his lekythoi, one of which (Boston 01.8079; see Plate 33) shows Eos and a fawn, the other (Boston 13.198) depicting a young hunter with his dog, are models of simplicity.

The Pan Painter was a follower of Myson. Others of Myson's followers, however, lacked the Pan Painter's ability, and their figures tended to be stiff and pretty, Archaic but stale. The *Pig Painter, Leningrad Painter,* and *Agrigento Painter* were better than the rest. (See Plate 34 for an example of the Pig Painter's work—a column-krater, Cleveland 24.197.) This group of mannerists concentrated on Myson's favorite shape, the column-krater. No potters' names are associated with these painters and only one of the group, the *Oinanthe Painter,* used any *kalos* names.

Followers of Makron also continued that Archaic master's style on cups, but in a smaller, mannered and petty form. The *Clinic Painter* and the *Telephos Painter* may be mentioned among these. The latter was the most mannered of the group, with cadaverous figures in angular poses. The potter Hieron worked with the Telephos Painter, and the *kalos* name Lichas is found on the latter's work. One other follower of Makron, the *Painter of Philadelphia 2449,* appears to have employed the *kalos* name Hiketes.

Inspiration from Murals

The *Niobid Painter* and his group, including notably the *Altamura, Blenheim, Wooly Satyrs, Geneva* and *Spreckels* painters are among those inspired by the mural paintings of Polygnotos and Nikon. They tended to employ large, crowded, elaborate compositions on large pots especially on volute-, calyx-, and bell-kraters. Their favorite scenes were battles of Greeks and Amazons, Lapiths against centaurs, and the fall of Troy. In their paintings, they made bold attemps at foreshortening and employed dilute washes to indicate shadows.

The Niobid Painter, whose work covers the years ca. 465–450 B.C., derives his sobriquet from his depiction of the death of Niobe's children on a calyx-krater (Louvre MNC 511 G 341; see Plate 35). He was by far the most ambitious of the group. His attributed 121 works are almost all large items including all types of kraters (except column-kraters, which he and all his group eschewed), hydriai, and amphorae. No potters' signatures are found on any of his works nor on any of the works of his group, and there are no *kalos* names on any of his vases. (Of his group, only the Spreckels Painter is known to have used any *kalos* name and he appears to have used one, the name Eualkos, only once.)

The Niobid Painter's name-piece is his most ambitious work; a late piece, it dates perhaps to ca. 455–450 B.C. This is the epitome of the early trend toward adapting mural art to vase painting. On this vase, a calyx-krater, he ranged his figures on varying levels over the whole field, indicating hilly ground by light lines; one figure is even half hidden behind a small hillock. There is some ambiguity as to whether the upper figures are merely on higher ground or farther away; in any case, they do not diminish in size. Some of the figures are depicted in quiet, dignified, statuesque poses in contrast to others which are contorted in pain or death. They thus evidence the self-composed elevation of spirit of the time combined with a new attempt to portray emotion and mood through posture rather than gesture. This vase, while almost certainly not copied from any of the great murals of the time, appears to embody the mural treatment of spatial relationships.

One of his earlier works, a volute-krater (Palermo G 1283), dating to ca. 460 B.C. or before, is more typical of the group. This depicts Lapiths and centaurs on the neck and a battle of Greeks and Amazons on the body, going all around the pot. The figures occupy the full height of both friezes and are set on base lines of tongues for the former and of meander for the latter.

Pre-Classicism

The chief exponent of the trend toward painting of quiet monumental scenes is the *Villa Giulia Painter*. He derives his name from a calyx-krater in Rome (Villa Giulia 909) depicting dancing women. Most of his attributed 123 works are large pots such as various krater forms, hydriai, and stamnoi, though he also decorated kylikes and such small items as lekythoi, including several white-ground items. No potters' names have been found on his work and he is known to have used only the *kalos* name Nikon. He employed calm, harmonious scenes with quiet, serene figures drawn with little imagination (see Plate 36 for one of his better bell-kraters, New York 24.97.96). Typical scenes show a bearded man holding a scepter, a woman holding a wine jug and a phiale, or pouring a libation for a departing warrior.

Another painter of this group is the *Chicago Painter*, who derives his name from a stamnos (Chicago 89.22) depicting women at a Dionysian festival. He has some forty-six attributed works, most of which are stamnoi, hydriai, pelikai, and various forms of kraters, though he also painted a few small items. No potter's name is associated with his work and he employed only Alkimachos and Chairis as *kalos* names. The Chicago Painter's style is similar to that of the Villa Giulia Painter, but is freer, livelier, and less statuesque.

The *Methyse Painter* belongs to the same school. His sobriquet comes from that of a maenad in a Dionysian procession depicted on one of his bell-kraters (New York 07.286.85). Though he has only twelve clearly attributed items, he is an important representative of the group. It is interesting to compare his stately Dionysian processions with the wild satyrs and ecstatic maenads of the Kleophrades Painter.

All three of these painters were followers of Douris. Other painters in the tradition of Douris, but decorating cups, also painted in the quiet monumental style depicting youths, satyrs, and schoolroom scenes of little action, drawn with delicate lines and expressing such moods as exaltation and reverence. Among these, mention may be made of the *Akestorides Painter*, the *Painter of Munich 2660*, the *Euaichme Painter* and the *Euaion Painter*. Two of these derive their names from *kalos* names (the Akestorides Painter and the Euaion Painter—the latter also used Nikon and the Euaichme Painter used Isthmodoros as *kalos* names). No potters' names have been found on any of their works.

Naturalism

The naturalist trend had its major exponents in the Pistoxenos Painter and the Penthesileia Painter, both cup painters, as were others of this group. As cup painters, they were essentially miniaturists. As naturalists, they sought to bring greater realism to an art which was threatened by the sterility of perfect, but spiritless pictures. Thus they used gestures and facial expressions to portray emotion, introduced realistic touches, employed shading to give roundness to their figures or applied additional colors in their red-figured work. Both of these painters tried their hand at white-ground work, where they could use a polychrome style. Their many followers appear to have been less venturesome, content to imitate one or the other of the two masters in red-figure, sometimes lapsing into reproduction of a series of repetitive scenes on their cups.

The *Pistoxenos Painter* derives his name from a skyphos (Schwerin 708; see Plate 37) signed by the potter Pistoxenos. One of his masterpieces, this skyphos shows the young Herakles and his nurse, Geropso, on one side, and Iphikles, half brother of Herakles, with the music teacher, Linos, on the other. Megakles and Euphronios also signed as potters on works by the Pixtoxenos Painter.[6]

Working in the years ca. 475–460, the Pixtoxenos Painter is credited with only thirty-nine items, thirty-two of which are stemmed kylikes; the others include three stemless kylikes, a covered cup, a pyxis, a bobbin and his famous skyphos. On his works are found the *kalos* names Glaukon and Lysis and the *kalé* name Heras. His work was once regarded as an early phase of the Penthesileia Painter, but now the two are considered to be distinct personalities.

His skyphos in Schwerin is illustrative of his naturalism and a masterpiece of characterization. The aged Geropso is shown with white hair, wrinkled skin, hooked nose, double chin, a one-tooth smile, shuffling along with a bent stick, and wearing shoes complete to laces. The young Herakles looks surly and sports an arrow-stick, leaving his nurse to carry his lyre. Linos also is clearly characterized: old, skinny, with white hair and sparse beard, he slumps in his chair appearing to watch Iphikles with spiteful ill-humor. In contrast, the boy sits straight on his stool apparently absorbed in the music. A kitharos hanging on the wall adds a touch of background realism to the scene. Despite the fidelity of such red-figured scenes to real life, the Pistoxenos Painter seems to have been impelled to look farther afield. Thus, his other masterpieces are done in white-ground on the interiors of four cups (see the next chapter).

The *Penthesileia Painter* began his career in the late sixties of the fifth century and continued on somewhat beyond mid-century. On a kylix interior (Munich 2688; see Plate 38), he depicted the death of the Amazon queen, Penthesileia—hence his name. This and another kylix tondo (Munich 2689) showing Apollo slaying Tityos are his masterpieces. In all, he has 183 attributed works, with 154 kylikes and the rest small items except for one hydria. No potters' names have been found on any of his works and among inscriptions, only one *kalé* name, Heras, is found, though the generic *Ho pais kalos* (the boy is fair) is frequent.

His namepiece serves to illustrate his efforts at naturalism. Though it is far more elaborate and crowded than most of his works, he successfully portrayed the emotion and mood of the poignant moment. In painting the scene, he employed various accessory colors: red-brown, yellow, gray-blue and white, with red and brown washes, and applied gilded clay. Most of these colors are now lost, but from remaining traces, it is evident that this kylix tondo must have been quite different from traditional red-figured work. Incidentally, this is one of the largest Type B kylikes ever found; a still larger one, also his work, found at Spina (Ferrara T.18), measures 72 cm. from handle to handle and depicts the deeds of Theseus inside and the fall of Troy outside.

On his slighter works, the Penthesileia Painter employed a rather spontaneous, sketchy style showing pursuits, satyrs and maenads, youths arming, with horses or at the palaestra, and departure scenes which are rhythmic and often vivacious. Like the Pistoxenos Painter, he experimented with white-ground (on three small items) employing a polychrome style. Though, as noted in the first chapter, collaboration of painters in the school of the Penthesileia Painter was frequent, he does not appear to have worked with any other painter in the decoration of any of his own vases.

Miscellaneous

Other painters of the early Classical period do not fit well into any of the four rather imprecise categories. Among these, *Hermonax* and the *Sabouroff Painter* stand out. The former continued the style of the Berlin Painter during the years ca. 470–450 B.C., and, unlike most of his contemporaries, was relatively successful in preserving the freshness and liveliness of the Archaic period. (See Plate 39, a stamnos by Hermonax, which is typical of his work, Boston 01.8031.) The Sabouroff Painter liked quiet designs; he was, however, at his best in white-ground, where he was a pioneer. Other painters of the period seem to have specialized in the production of Nolan amphorae, lekythoi, alabastra, or skyphoi. Some of these were followers of the Kleophrades Painter and others of the Berlin Painter or Onesimos.

CLASSICAL FREE STYLE ca. 450–420 B.C.

The period of Perikles' administration in Athens (449–429 B.C.) encompasses years in which that city-state was at the height of its power and wealth. Beginning of construction of the Parthenon in 447/6 B.C. epitomized the great effort put into rebuilding and beautification of the city. Architecture, sculpture and relief work flowered under such master architects as Iktinos and Kallikrates and such master sculptors as Pheidias, while in the field of mural painting, Polygnotos of Thasos and Nikon remained active. Some artists, who under other circumstances, might have done vase painting, sought expression in these fields. A few great artists continued in the special art of vase painting, but most of the painters were of second rank and many tended to become mere decorators.

The spirit of the times called for portrayal of idealized human beauty and dignity in line with the sculptures of Pheidias. Thus, old scenes of strife and action were toned down even more than before. Dionysian revels became calm processions, scenes of drunken carousals were replaced by quiet groups with two figures standing or sitting, listening to music, conversing, or contemplating. Battle scenes were displaced by those of wives bidding farewell to warrior husbands. In brief, the ribald and brutal were almost eliminated.

By the mid-fifth century B.C., drawing of the human body and its drapery had been fully mastered.[7] Though the profile head remained the favorite, full frontal and three-quarter views were relatively common. Depiction of hair appears to have depended more on the whim of the artist than on any conventions, being shown as a black mass, as fluffy curls, or as separate strands against a reserved background. The most important development was in depiction of the eye. This first became truly profile, as the pupil was omitted and the iris elongated, usually touching only the upper eyelid, and then drawn as a solid black triangle. Drawing the upper lid with two lines and addition of one or two curves for eyelashes completed the process of creating a realistic eye in a profile face.

By its reliance on sharp outline drawing, the red-figure technique was less well adapted than white-ground for depiction of the human body. Red-figure artists, however, attained roundness of form by shading and the stately poses of classical art lessened the problem of showing torsion. Drapery, in consonance with classical sculpture, was drawn in flowing lines, curving to follow the shape of the body and falling in natural lines with the stance or motion of the figures; thin washes were often employed to enhance the illusion of shadows and depth of folds.

Despite the attractions offered by other fields of art, more than two hundred artists are listed by Beazley as working in the years ca. 450–420 B.C.[8] As noted above, however, there were fewer first rate artists.

The best of these artists are followers of late Archaic or early Classical masters, though they developed their own styles in red-figure, which carried them away from their masters into more subdued and classical ideals of quiet dignity. Some turned to the white-ground technique, which became a major competitor of the red-figure technique.

Archaism: The Late Mannerists

About ten painters have been identified as "late mannerists." Like their earlier counterparts, they sought to continue painting in the Archaic style and, like them, they appear to have specialized primarily in column-kraters. None of them with the possible exception of the *Nausikaa Painter*[9] is of major importance. They are of interest primarily for their deliberate pursuit of archaism.

Inspiration from Murals and Sculpture

Polygnotos was an outstanding vase painter during the years ca. 445–430 B.C. Strictly a vase painter, he is not to be confused with the great muralist, Polygnotos of Thasos.[10] His name is known from his signature on five items.[11] No potters' names are found on his works. He used the *kalos* name Nikomas and, possibly Nikodemos (i.e., not followed by *kalos*). He is an heir to the grand style of the Niobid Painter, but like others of the period was affected by the sculpture of Pheidias, especially in his idealization of human faces and figures, the refined perfection of drapery, and the air of lassitude of his characters. His figures, though well-rounded, are somewhat weak and expressionless, while his scenes are rather commonplace. His total seventy-one attributed works are on large items including stamnoi, various types of kraters (except column-kraters), neck-amphorae, hydriai, and the like.

His five signed items along with an unsigned pelike (New York 45.11.1) are among his best works. These items depict such scenes as centauromachies, amazonomachies, and the deeds of Herakles, Achilles, and Perseus. One of these is his stamnos in London (96.7-16.5; see Plate 40) showing Herakles and a centaur. As an example of how tastes had changed, his New York pelike with the death of Medusa avoids picturing the actual death, and simply shows Perseus with his sword drawn standing over Medusa. The legendary gorgon is portrayed as a sleeping woman, with neither the snakes nor the horrifying visage common in Archaic art. Others of his favorite scenes include those with Apollo and Dionysos as well as musicals and libations.

His immediate following numbers about fourteen painters and groups. Of these, the most distinguished is the *Lykaon Painter*, while the *Christie Painter* is the most prolific. Others include the *Hektor, Peleus, Coghill, Epimedes* and *Pantoxena* painters. There are, in addition, a fairly large number of stamnoi, kraters, amphorae, and other large pots, embracing some very good pieces done by artists of his group who have not been specifically identified. *Kalos* names found on vases of the Polygnotan group include Alkimachos, Axiopeithes, Epimedes, Euaion, Eunikos, Kallias, Megakles and Polymainetes. *Kalé* names include Hediste, Kleitagora, Kleophonis, and Pantoxena.

Classicism

The *Achilles Painter* began to paint during the last ten years of the early classical period, but worked on into the 430s B.C. A pupil of the Berlin Painter, he continued that Archaic master's style. His early work is very close to that of the Berlin Painter and at one time was attributed to the "Meletos Painter" from his frequent use of that *kalos* name. This early work is notable for its sketchy, summary style of drawing and vivid characterization of figures. Once his style was established, he became the most important exponent of portrayal of simple, dignified human beauty in the full Classical spirit. His mature style is extremely uniform, usually depicting one figure beautifully done on the obverses of his works and stock figures of mantled youths on the reverses—as Miss Richter notes, "The mantled figures on the reverses of his vases serve almost as a trademark of his work."[12] His namepiece, a Type B amphora (Vatican from Vulci; see Plate 41) dated between ca. 450 and 440 B.C., a product of his mature period, is an exception to this "trademark." On the obverse, is the hero, Achilles (name inscribed). On the reverse, is a woman, probably Briseis. Both are in free field, standing only on a band of meander in the spotlight manner reminiscent of the Berlin Painter. Indeed, many of his works are characterized by such isolated figures spot-lit against the black background. The figures on the obverse sides are almost always beautifully drawn in quiet, serene poses fully within the spirit of Pheidian sculpture of the Periklean age.

In all, he has 233 attributed works, 126 in red-figure, 101 in white-ground on lekythoi and six prize Panathenaic amphorae done in the traditional black-figure technique.

His red-figured works include both large and small pots such as large neck-amphorae, small Nolan amphorae, calyx- and bell-kraters, hydriai, stamnoi, oinochoai, and many lekythoi. (Plate 42, a Nolan type neck-amphora, New York 12.236.2, is typical of his red-figured work.)

No potters' names are found on any of his works, however, he used inscriptions to name his characters or favorites of the time.[13]

When he turned to white-ground lekythoi, he became the leading painter in this technique.

As noted in the introduction, he collaborated with the Sabouroff Painter in decorating a loutrophoros (Philadelphia 30.4.1; see Plate 43). His large red-figured works tend to show Dionysian scenes and the deeds of Theseus, whereas his small red-figured lekythoi depict mythological subjects, and, sometimes, funerary scenes.

Among close followers of the Achilles Painter in the red-figure technique we may list the *Dwarf Painter,* the *Persephone Painter* and the *Painter of the Boston Phiale.* The first used the *kalos* name, Dion, and the last the name, Euaion; none of their works have potters' signatures. In addition to these, six other red-figure and a number of white-ground painters are closely associated with the master.

Other classicists of the period are followers of the Villa Giulia Painter. Foremost among these was the *Mannheim Painter.* He had a fine sense of composition and placed beautifully drawn, somewhat formal figures in quiet, dignified poses. His name is derived from an oinochoe (Mannheim 61), which is one of twelve of these shapes with which he is credited (he has only one other attributed item, a pot fragment). (One of his best vases is shown in Plate 44; New York 06.1021.189.) No potters' names or *kalos* names have been found on any of his works.

Other followers of the Villa Giulia Painter include the *Eupolis Painter,* the *Kleio Painter,* the *Cassel Painter,* the *Danae Painter* and the *Menelaos Painter.* The potters working with these painters did not sign their works and none of these painters employed *kalos* or *kalé* names.

Exquisiteness

Though obviously influenced by the sculpture of Pheidias, certain cup painters of the free Classical period—perhaps because they were miniaturists—seem to have turned to extreme delicacy and to the exquisite.

The *Eretria Painter,* one of the most able painters of kylikes and small pots during the years ca. 430–420 B.C., is an example. The item for which he is named is an onos (or epinetron) found in Eretria, now in the Athens National Museum (Athens 1629); it depicts Alkestis in her bridal chamber preparing for her wedding. The Eretria Painter's attributed 110 works have been found widely dispersed in Greece, Italy, Spain, and southern Russia. Fifty-eight of these are kylikes[14] and practically all the rest are small vessels. Incidentally, his best work seems to have been on small pots rather than on kylikes. (The squat lekythos, New York 30.11.8, shown in Plate 45 is a fine example of his work.)

He worked at least with the potter, Epigenes, who signed one of his works, a kantharos in Paris (Cab. Med. 851).

He used the *kalos* names Alkimachos (without *kalos*) and Kallias as well as frequent inscriptions to identify his characters.

Rejecting classical severity, he turned to delicacy and prettiness, tending to embellish his work with ornaments in gilded clay. His figures have delicate, gentle faces, soft curling hair and beautifully drawn hands. They wear clinging garments, often depicted as transparent, and drawn with numerous flowing lines. There is an air of overrefinement, effeminacy, and playful charm in much of his work which looks ahead to later works by the Meidias Painter.

Though he is not known to have painted any of the usual white-ground shoulder lekythoi of the period, he occasionally worked in polychrome on a white background. A white-ground squat lekythos (Kansas City 31.80) and another of the same shape (New York 31.11.13), which has three zones, the middle in white-ground and the other two in red-figure, are known examples.

Other cup painters of this same group include notably the *Kodros Painter*, a distinguished artist, reflecting Pheidian idealism in exquisitely refined detail, and the *Kraipale Painter*, whose restraint and serenity is similarly evident in the delicacy of his work.

There were, of course, many other painters of cups and small pots during this period, but to detail them would be both tedious and unprofitable.

SUMMARY

In this chapter, we have seen how various artists attempted to carry the red-figure technique beyond its natural apex into the Classical period. Given the near exhaustion of the red-figure technique coupled with competition and influences from other art forms, we have followed various solutions attempted by red-figure painters of the period. We have seen that success or failure of these vase painters depended more on their individual abilities than on the avenue of their solution.

In the next chapter, we shall consider those painters who sought solution to their problems in a different technique and then return, in the last chapter, to the decline and extinction of the red-figure technique.

Notes on V—The Red-figure Technique in Crisis

1. See Appendix II, Figures A12-A14, A29-A31, A52-A54 and A63-A66 for illustrations of head, hair, eye, body and drapery.

2. *ARV*; some of these I have considered in Chapter VI.

3. Beazley, *ARV*, p. 361.

4. Robertson, *Greek Painting*, p. 120.

5. Cook, *Greek P. P.*, p. 180.

6. A cup with a white-ground interior (Berlin 2282) bears the signature of Euphronios and is the latest of his works as potter. Two other fragmentary cups, also with white-ground interiors (Athens Acr. 439 and Taranto from Locri) were once signed and, by analogy with the Berlin cup, are regarded as having been potted by Euphronios.

7. See Appendix II, Figures A15, A16, A32-A34 and A67-A68 for illustrations of the human body and its drapery.

8. *ARV* as amended by *Paralipomena*. Some of these I have included in Chapters VI and VII.

9. The Nausikaa Painter derives his name from his depiction of Nausikaa and Odysseus on a neck-amphora (Munich 2322); his real name is Polygnotos as is known from his *egrapsen* signature on an amphora (London E 284).

10. Polygnotos appears to have been a fairly common name at this time. Thus, the Nausikaa Painter and the Lewis Painter both signed works with this name and a fragmentary inscription on a calyx-krater in Munich by one of the Group of Polygnotos may be the signature of a fourth painter by this name.

11. Two stamnoi (Brussels A 134 and London 96.7-16.5), a bell-krater (Reggio, no number), a neck-amphora (Moscow Hist. Mus. Inv. 73) and a pelike (Syracuse 23507).

12. Richter, *Survey*, p. 118. From about this time it is appropriate to speak of the "front" and the "back" of vases with the former well done and the latter cursory at best.

13. On his red-figured works he used the following *kalos* names: Alkaios, Axiopeithes, Euaion, Hegeleos; Kleinias, son of Pedieus; Lichas, son of Samieus and Meletos.

14. Some of his kylikes were previously attributed to the "Lemnos Painter."

VI

The White-Ground Technique:
Another Attempted Solution[1]

BACKGROUND

The white-ground technique[2] involved polychrome painting against a white slip background. It became important in the 460s B.C., apparently, when artists sought greater naturalism for their work than permitted by the red-figure technique. In its developed form, white-ground work was clearly influenced by the paintings of the great muralists of the last two-thirds of the fifth century B.C. and came closer than either black-figure or red-figure to then-contemporary wall and panel paintings.[3] This relationship is to be found in the employment of a *light background, outline drawing* and in variety of *colors* as employed by the muralists.

Light backgrounds are found on Cretan and Mycenaean pottery. Pale slips, yellowish to cream, on which designs were painted had been used on some Attic pottery from the Protogeometric to the early Geometric period and had been used again in the Proto-Attic period.[4] Slips of varying degrees of white also had been employed throughout much of the Archaic period in non-Attic styles—notably on Chiot, Rhodian and Laconian pottery. In the second quarter of the sixth century, an Attic painter, Nearchos, had experimented with a white background for a band of black and red tongues on the lip of a kantharos (Athens Acr. 611), but this experiment failed and other Attic painters of the time painted red and black directly on the clay ground. None of these forerunners appear to have had any very direct connection with the chalky-white coating which became popular during the late sixth century in Attic black-figure nor with the white-ground work of the red-figure period.

Outline drawing had characterized Proto-Attic painting on pottery of the seventh century B.C., but had been replaced by the silhouette of the black-figure technique by the end of that century. Throughout the sixth century B.C., however, outline drawing had persisted "as a thin trickle side by side with the broad stream of black-figure."[5] For instance, Sophilos and Nearchos outlined white horses teamed with black silhouette horses[6] and it was common to paint the flesh of women white outlined in black. The Amasis Painter even drew females in outline against the orange-red background.[7]

During the late sixth century and the first part of the fifth century B.C., outline drawing became somewhat more common especially on black-figured shoulder lekythoi with white backgrounds. A few painters, including the Sappho Painter, the Diosphos Painter, and some unidentified painters in the workshop of the Bowdoin Painter, drew outline figures alongside silhouette figures or drew figures partly in outline and partly in silhouette in what is known as "semi-outline."

The red-figure technique, of course, involved outline drawing, but the effect was lost when the black of the outline merged into the black of the background. However, when red-figure painters employed a white background for their work, the outline immediately became an apparent and important feature.

The *variety of colors* employed for white-ground work also contrasts with the use of colors in the other two techniques. In black-figure, colors had been limited to the orange-red of the background, the black of the silhouette and white, plus various shades of red and purple for minor features. Black-figure work against a white background, which employed the black silhouette without use of other colors, thus remained a sub-specie of the black-figure technique. Red-figure was essentially a two color technique in which only occasional use was made of white and red (until, in its decline, a variety of colors was added). In white-ground, many colors, both fast and fugitive, were employed including yellow, green, blue, mauve, pink and a variety of reds.

True white-ground work evolved slowly. At first, it must have been employed simply as a variant like the black-figured white background work and for the same reason that artists sometimes did bilingual items—to provide interesting contrasts.

White-ground thus appears, at first, as an experimental sideline, adopted by red-figure artists for oinochoai, alabastra, and other small items and for the inside of cups. The semi-outline drawing, mentioned earlier, perhaps marks the beginning of later specialization on shoulder lekythoi.[8] At first, few colors were employed against the white background, but as time went on, more colors were added. Initially, white-ground vases were made for use in the home, but as new and often fugitive colors were added, the technique became unsuitable for such daily wear. The shape employed became confined almost exclusively to the shoulder lekythos. Its use became primarily funerary and specialists appeared who painted only in this technique.

Because of its closeness to painting on walls, panels, and on less durable fabrics, some writers regard the best white-ground work as the purest remaining expressions of classical art;[9] others treat it as an outgrowth of the red-figure technique.[10] In any case, it was produced in great volume after the middle of the fifth century B.C., especially in the last quarter of that century and comprises a second major vase painting technique of classical Athens. As such it deserves special consideration.

RED-FIGURE PAINTERS
EMPLOYING WHITE BACKGROUND
ca. 530–475 B.C.

In Chapter III, we noted that two of the very earliest red-figure artists experimented in the use of white. The *Andokides Painter*, it will be recalled, employed a white slip for female figures drawn on a small red-figured amphora (Louvre F. 203) and as background on the lip of an amphora (New York 63.11.6) for black-figured depictions of Herakles and the Nemean Lion.[11] We noted also that *Psiax* employed a white background for black silhouette figures on one of his alabastra (Leningrad 381). From a few years later, are two plaques, one showing a warrior (Acropolis Mus. 1037) and the other the goddess Athena (Acropolis Mus. 2590 and Oxford 1927.4602 fr.).[12] The style of the warrior plaque, which is almost complete, is closely related to that of Euthymides. This plaque has a light background against which the warrior is in brown with painted muscular details, though his robe is black with incised folds. His helmet and shield are drawn in outline.

Originally, the plaque was inscribed "Megakles *kalos*," but the name later was partially erased and Glaukytes substituted (probably echoing the political exile of the former). The Athena plaque is so fragmentary that firm attribution is even more difficult, but it also is related to Euthymides. This shows the goddess with white skin outlined in black with details mostly painted instead of incised.

Other examples of early work by red-figure painters on white background include three alabastra[13] in the manner of the Euergides Painter (signed *Pasiades epoiesen*) and a fragmentary lekythos (Athens Agora NS AP 422) with *Pasiades egrapsen*, which is the only known painter's signature on a white-ground lekythos.

It will be seen that prior to the end of the sixth century, work by red-figure painters on a white background was rare and apparently experimental.

In Chapter IV, we saw that the *Brygos Painter* did at least one white-ground lekythos (*Gela, ex Navarra Jacona*) and painted the inside of one of his best kylikes on white-ground (Munich 2645). *Douris* also is credited with one white-ground work, a lekythos (Cleveland 66.114). In this same period, ca. 500 to 475 B.C., the *Skyriskos Painter* did a white-ground lekythos (Berlin 2252), and various minor painters worked with lekythoi, alabastra, oinochoai, and plates with surfaces of white.

Since the potentialities of the red-figure technique were by no means exhausted, late Archaic artists appear to have used white-ground work as an expression of individualism.

At first, figures were outlined in the concentrated solution which fired shiny black. Gradually, a dilute solution came into use. This fired a lustrous golden-brown or golden-yellow and is known as "glaze outline."[14]

EARLY CLASSICAL WHITE-GROUND ca. 475–450 B.C.

In Chapter V, we suggested that various artists of the early Classical period apparently turned to work in white-ground as a new means of expression in the art of vase painting. Among major painters, the *Villa Giulia Painter* tried his hand with two white-ground lekythoi (both at Lugano in the Schoen Collection) and four white-ground alabastra.[15] The *Penthesileia Painter* produced in white-ground two bobbins (New York 28.167 and Athens Ceramicos Mus. no number) and one pyxis (New York 07.286.36). The latter item, showing the Judgment of Paris, is a chaming example of the painter's ability to convey an air of realism and ranks among his masterpieces (see Plate 46).[16] About a dozen other red-figure painters experimented with white-ground work in these years. Among them, five, at least, warrant mention: the *Bowdoin Painter*, the *Aischines Painter*, the *Carlsruhe Painter*, the *Providence Painter* and the *Ikaros Painter*. These artists produced some 150 white-ground items, many of excellent quality.

The *Pistoxenos Painter* was more pioneer than experimenter in the new technique. Aside from his red-figured skyphos in Schwerin, his masterpieces are four cup interiors done in white-ground. Of these, the most complete (London D 2) depicts a regal Aphrodite (name inscribed) riding through the air on a goose. The others (Berlin 2282, Athens Acr. 439 and Taranto from Locri) show respectively Achilles and Diomedes, the Death of Orpheus, and a satyr with a maenad. On the Berlin cup, he employed the black relief line to outline his figures, but on the others he used the golden-brown dilute glaze. Interestingly, he employed an additional snowy white for the flesh of women on some of his works.

The *Sabouroff Painter*, with some 122 white-ground lekythoi among his total 289 attributed works, is one of the most important workers in the new technique. His name is derived from a red-figured nuptial lebes in Berlin, originally from the Sabouroff collection (Berlin 2404). His best work, however, is in white-ground. Perhaps, his masterpiece is a superb Hera on a kylix interior (Munich 2685), but he has many lovely scenes, most of them relating to death, on lekythoi—men or women listening to music, making offerings, or mourning beside a tomb. At first, he appears to have used shiny black or golden-brown dilute glaze lines for his outlines, but he soon turned to matte black for most of his outlines.

The *Sotades Painter*, named after the potter with whom he worked, has only twenty attributed vases and of these, only three are in white-ground, but each of these is worthy of special note. These include a stemless cup (London D 7) and two stemmed kylikes (London D 5 and London D 6). All three are very small and delicate with wishbone handles. Though only one (London

D 6), is certainly signed by the potter Sotades, the other two are clearly his work. The stemless cup, though fragmentary, shows a man fleeing from a monstrous snake (sometimes interpreted as the death of Opheltos). One of the stemmed kylikes (London D 5) illustrates the story of how a magician, Polyidos, brought Glaukos, son of King Minos of Crete, back to life. The other kylix (London D 6) is a particularly charming fragment showing a girl in three-quarter view on tiptoe picking an apple from near the top of a small tree. Done in the golden-brown dilute glaze outline with added colors, these pieces are regarded as among the finest reflections of the mural art of that period.

In Chapter V, we also noted that some early Classical painters began to specialize in the white-ground technique and to concentrate on the lekythos form. Among almost a score of such specialists, we may pick out the *Tymbos Painter* with 105 attributed works and the *Inscription Painter* with fifteen attributed items as amongst the best representatives of the group.

Most of the white-ground work of this period was made for use in the home on lekythoi, alabastra, pyxides, and the interiors of kylikes. A few painters, including the Sabouroff Painter and the Inscription Painter included funerary scenes, anticipating the development which soon was to dominate all white-ground work.

We have seen how shiny black lines were replaced by golden-brown dilute outlines during these years and then how matte black and red gradually began to supplant the glaze outlines. Solid areas, in general, such as drapery and inanimate objects were filled in with brownish or purplish reds.

CLASSICAL WHITE-GROUND ca. 450–430 B.C.

By mid-fifth century, the white-ground technique was fully established as a major competitor of the red-figure technique. Some painters still worked in both techniques, but the group of specialists had grown and production of the white-ground shoulder lekythos rivaled that of any other single shape.

The *Achilles Painter* is credited with having given new status and direction to the white-ground shoulder lekythos, about the middle of the fifth century, as a result of his superb production of more than one hundred of these vases.[17] Thereafter, white-ground work became almost entirely confined to the shoulder lekythos. Furthermore, the form became almost exclusively funerary in use, despite the fact that the Achilles Painter's early items do not depict scenes clearly connected with the grave. Interestingly, he seems to have resisted replacement of the golden-brown dilute by matte colors for his outlines until late in his career (at least 92 of his works are in glaze outline). Similarly, on his early work, he employed added snowy white on top of the white background for details and for the flesh of women, though he abandoned this too in his later work.

It is his work on white-ground lekythoi that makes the Achilles Painter a really great artist.[18] Among his many fine works, it is difficult to single out the most outstanding. A few may be mentioned as among his masterpieces. His depiction of a warrior departing for battle, saying farewell to his wife (Athens 1818) conveys an air of quiet pathos seldom matched. A scene showing two muses, one seated on a rock playing a kithara and the other standing, with a small bird between them, is beautifully preserved (Schoen Coll. in Lugano). The colors on this vase are almost intact, including yellow, vermillion, wine-red, reddish-brown, and black in addition to the white of the background (only the color of the undergarment on the shoulder of the standing muse has been lost). Another masterpiece (Boston 13.201) shows a woman, probably a servant, holding out a stool to her mistress, the figures are epitomes of classical calm (see Plate 47, in which outline is in golden brown dilute; in Plate 48, New York 07.286.42, the outlines are matte).

No potters' names are found on any of the Achilles Painter's white-ground lekythoi. As noted in Chapter V, he employed *kalos* names on his white-ground works,[19] and on the Lugano vase mentioned above he included a very rare place name with the inscription *Helicon*.

During these same years, ca. 450–420 B.C., a few good red-figure painters worked occasionally in white-ground and in some cases turned out very fine pieces. Among these, may be listed the *Painter of Munich 2335*, the *Phiale Painter*, the *Dessypri Painter*, the *Klugmann Painter* and the *Eupolis Painter*. Even the *Eretria Painter* tried his hand at this technique, as we have seen in Chapter V. The trend, however, was toward specialization in the production of funerary lekythoi.

At least a score of identified painters of the free classical period appear to have specialized entirely in white-ground work. Of these, four may serve as illustrations. (Typical white-ground lekythoi by the first three of these artists are shown in Plates 49 to 51 [New York 23.160.38, London D 58, and Fogg 1925, 30.54 respectively.]) The *Bosanquet Painter* (named after R. C. Bosanquet, an archaeologist of the late 19th century) has eleven attributed works, of which all but one are white-ground lekythoi. The *Thanatos Painter* (a sobriquet derived from his depiction of Thanatos and Hypnos on a white-ground lekythos, London D 58) has forty-nine of these special lekythoi attributed to him. Of these, thirty-nine have glaze outlines, and the rest have matte outlines. The *Bird Painter* (named from a bird on Athens 1769) is credited with thirty-nine white-ground lekythoi—six in glaze and the rest in matte outline. The *Quadrate Painter* (so-called from the chequer-squares used on his meanders) has an attributed seventy-six white-ground lekythoi—with only ten in glaze outline and sixty-six with matte outlines.

As will be noted, the glaze outline was rapidly abandoned in favor of matte red or black or a combination of the two for outline drawing.[20] Similarly, new colors were added at this time for solid areas. These included, first, several reds,[21] plus matte ochreyellow, and later, rose-red, vermillion, pink, sky-blue, matte black and light purple.[22] The additional snowy white for the flesh of women was largely abandoned in this period. Introduction of these fugitive colors was one reason lekythoi came to be used almost exclusively for funerary purposes—the colors simply could not withstand ordinary wear.

With the establishment of the white lekythos as the main funerary item of pottery, the scenes depicted became more appropriate for the grave.[23] Favorites included: a lady and her maid, a soldier's farewell to his wife, visits to the grave, the laying out of the dead, and incidents of the other world such as Charon and his boat, Hermes guiding the dead, or Sleep and Death carrying away the body. The Achilles Painter, for example, depicted slender, fine-boned men and women standing or sitting while looking at each other in silent, often melancholy, understanding. His immediate companions, the Thanatos and Bosanquet painters, also produced quiet, subdued art. Other followers, the Phiale Painter, the Bird Painter and the Painter of Munich 2335, tended to produce more tender and melancholy scenes with pathetically childish children.

LATE FIFTH CENTURY
WHITE-GROUND ca. 430–400 B.C.

Against the background of the great plague (430/29 B.C.) and the disastrous events of the Peloponnesian War, it is not surprising to find Athenian production of funerary white-ground lekythoi of increasing importance relative to normal trade items done in red-figure. The white-ground vases of this period are almost entirely the work of specialists,[24] of whom fifteen or more have been identified and given names. The style of these late specialists is far removed from the earlier subtle expressions of grief, being characterized instead by depictions of wild anguish, tearing of hair and descent to bathos, or by a heaviness of atmosphere and an air of great weariness. At the same time, new and highly fugitive colors were added and workmanship declined in quality.

Four painters will serve to illustrate these specialists. All appear to have worked only with shoulder lekythoi and to have employed matte outlines of red or black for their figures. The *Woman Painter* (so-called from his female figures) has twenty-six attributed works on which he depicted women in storms of lamentation and wild expressions of grief, using washes of blue, purple, green, mauve, yellow, and various reds. One of his better works is a lekythos in Athens (NM 1956; see Plate 52) depicting a young woman seated at her tomb with two friends.

The *Reed Painter* (named from the reeds common to his paintings of Charon conveying the dead across the river Styx) was more prolific with 156 attributed items, most of which are rather hackneyed and trite. Twenty-two items closely associated with the Reed Painter are collectively assigned to *Group R*. Two frequently illustrated lekythoi by Group R (Athens NM 1816 and Athens (NM 1817) show similar young warriors seated at the bases of grave stelae. The figures are heavy, weary, and sad with none of the grace, lightness, and confidence of earlier warrior figures (see Plate 53 for Athens NM 1816).

The *Triglyph Painter* (his work is characterized by three vertical lines on grave stelae depicted on his vases) has some fifty attributed works, many on very large lekythoi in a style that is overblown and empty.

With the work of these painters, we come to the end of the

white-ground technique about the close of the fifth century B.C. Not only did white-ground work die out, but the shoulder lekythos also disappeared as an item of painted pottery.

SUMMARY

In this chapter we have seen how early embellishment or experimentation with white on red-figured works developed into a new technique employed by artists seeking an alternative to the red-figure technique. Some of these artists were more successful than others, but in the long run, failure as vase painting was inevitable, once unfired and fugitive colors were employed. The horrors of the plague and disasters of war merely hastened the decline of this art form.

Notes on VI—The White-ground Technique

1. This chapter is based primarily on the following works: John Davidson Beazley, *Attic White Lekythoi*, (London: Oxford University Press, Humphrey Milford, 1938, hereafter cited as *AWL*), Arthur Fairbanks, *Athenian Lekythoi With Outline Drawing in Glaze Varnish on a White Ground*, (New York: McMillan Co., 1907), idem., *Athenian Lekythoi With Outline Drawing in Matt Color on a White Ground*, (New York: McMillan Co., 1914), Cook, *Greek P. P.,* Arias and Hirmer, *Greek Vase Painting,* Richter, *Survey* and Robertson, *Greek Painting.*

2. By convention, the term "white-ground" excludes black-figure painting against a white background. Cook, *Greek P. P.,* p. 178.

3. Robertson, *Greek Painting,* pp. 120ff and Richter, *Survey,* p. 93.

4. Cook, *Greek P. P.,* p. 177.

5. Beazley, *AWL,* p. 3, idem., *Attic Black-figure: A Sketch,* (London: Humphrey Milford Amen House E.C., 1930), p. 22 and Richter, *Survey,* p. 31.

6. For example, the horses of Sophilos on a dinos fragment (Athens 15499) and of Nearchos on a kantharos fragment (Athens Acr. 611).

7. For example, the women on the neck-amphora by the Amasis Painter in Paris (Cab. Med. 222).

8. Richter, *Survey,* p. 75, makes this suggestion.

9. See Cook, *Greek P. P.,* p. 182. Roberston, *Greek Painting,* by his emphasis on white-ground work, also seems to regard it very highly.

10. From the broad view of the history of painting, it is certainly true that white-ground works now provide us with some of the best indications of what mural and panel paintings looked like. On the other hand, from the narrower viewpoint of vase painting, white-ground work fails to meet the criteria of durability, permanence of colors and, hence, of utility.

11. Citing these two examples, and noting that the chalky white background of late sixth century Attic work bore little relation to the white slips employed elsewhere in Greece, Dietrich von Bothner has suggested that the Andokides Painter, perhaps, should be credited with the invention of the white-ground technique. (See his article on the Andokides potter and painter in the *Bulletin* of the Metropolitan Museum of Art, 1966.)

12. Robertson, *Greek Painting*, pp. 94-95 and John Boardman, *Greek Art*, (New York and Washington, Frederick A. Praeger Inc., 1965), p. 106.

13. London B 668, Athens 15002, and Louvre CA 1921. The first two are by the Pasiades Painter; the third may be by another artist.

14. Though, in fact, temperatures in Greek kilns did not reach the point at which the silica of the dilute solution fused into a true glaze, the term "glaze outline" has been in use for many years and, as Noble points out, the translucent lines may be referred to quite properly as a dilute glaze; Noble, *Attic P. P.*, p. 161.

15. Louvre MNC 627, Taranto 4536 (8284), Athens Agora Mus. 5233 and Giessen Univ. (no number).

16. Richter, *Survey*, p. 98 and von Bothmer, *Bulletin*, 1972.

17. Arias and Hirmer, *Greek Vase Painting*, p. 359.

18. Robertson, *Greek Painting*, p. 140.

19. On his white-ground works, he used the *kalos* names: Alkimedes, son of Aischylides; Axiopeithes, son of Alkimachos; Diphilos, son of Melanopos; Dromippos, son of Dromokleides; Hygiainon, and Pistoxenos, son of Aresandros.

20. The lustrous black and golden-brown were fired and completely fast colors. The matte colors were not fast; the matte red is better than the matte black, which fades to gray.

21. These sober reds were relatively fast.

22. All these other colors were fugitive and were applied after firing of the pot, since, unlike the clay paint and its dilutes, they could not withstand the heat of the kiln.

23. Interestingly, funerary white-ground lekythoi have been found only in Attica and in the Athenian settlement in Eretria where Athenian funerary customs were also observed. Arias and Hirmer, *Greek Vase Painting*, p. 359.

24. Occasionally, a red-figure painter ventured into this field. Thus, the Meidias Painter (*infra*) produced at least one white-ground lekythos.

VII

Decline of the Red-Figure Technique

LATE FIFTH CENTURY ca. 420–390 B.C.

The Peloponnesian War so interrupted the economic life and trade of Athens that its effects were felt even in the declining art of vase painting. The number of identified painters working in the period ca. 420–390 B.C., for example, is about half the number of those in the preceeding thirty years.[1] Some of the pottery workshops of the city may have been closed down.[2] In any case, output was greatly reduced as markets were lost with the decline of Athenian influence and loss of naval supremacy.

As we have seen in Chapter VI, the mood of the period was reflected in late white-ground lekythoi by heaviness and melancholy scenes. Red-figure painting of the period though less dejected, seems to be turned inward toward domestic life, lacking the confidence and heroism of earlier works. Increasing liberation of women appears to have had its influence also, as painters sought to attract this new clientele. Evidence of this may be found as scenes of the boudoir, of the myths of Dionysos with docile satyrs or of Aphrodite and her retinue, became increasingly more prevalent.

Among painters of the transition period from the free Classical style to that of the late fifth century, some continued to follow the classicism of the earlier period, while others further embellished the exquisite style of the late Classical cup painters. The general trend, however, was toward development of an ornate style, which in detail often was very fine, but which had an over-elaborate general effect.

151

That detail should be excellent is not surprising since mastery of drawing had long since been achieved. Profile heads remained most prevalent, but frontal and three-quarter views were common and done with ease. With some exceptions, hair was painted as separate strands or locks. The profile eye continued to be drawn convincingly, often with the lower lid shorter than the upper. Human figures tended to be either fleshy and heavy or increasingly effeminate, while shading and foreshortening became commonplace. Drapery was depicted usually either as heavy and flowing with only a few lines of contour or as diaphanous with multitudinous clinging folds.[3] During this period, subsidiary ornamentation was employed somewhat more discreetly than previously or later. On the more ornate vessels, use of white, yellow and applied gilded clay became usual. Buildings, furniture and other objects frequently were drawn in linear perspective. Use of *kalos* and *kalé* names declined sharply (only two of each are known) and only five potters bothered to sign their works. Of painters, we know the names of perhaps four.

The Classic Tradition

Among late followers in the classical tradition, who belong to the transition between the free Classical style and the ornate style of the late fifth century, are several painters of note.

The *Kleophon Painter* seems to have worked in the years ca. 435–420 B.C. Thus, on chronological grounds, he should have been placed in Chapter V. On the other hand, he is the first of a group of late followers of Polygnotos and has many ties with them. He derives his sobriquet from the use of Kleophon *kalos* on a stamnos (Leningrad 810); he also used the *kalos* name Megakles and from time to time the words *kalos* or *kalé* alone; no potters' names have been found on any of his works. His classicism is clearly evident in his serenely idealized figures and Pheidian influence is apparent in the lines of his drapery, but his figures are fleshier and more fluid than those of his predecessors.

Painting in a monumental style primarily on large vases (various types of kraters, hydriai, stamnoi and pelikai), his compositions are characterized by harmonious equilibrium, combined with an air of dreamy tranquility. Among sixty-nine attributed works, his stamnos (Munich 2415), showing a warrior saying farewell to his wife, is a beautiful example of how he could retain an air of serenity even in a situation of pathos (see Plate 54).

Another great painter in the classical tradition of Polygnotos was the *Dinos Painter*,[4] who derives his name from a famous dinos in East Berlin (Berlin F 2402; see Plate 55). Apparently a pupil of the Kleophon Painter, he worked in the last two decades of the fifth century B.C. Like his master, he was a painter of monumental figures on large vases (of his attributed forty-nine items, most are kraters of the calyx or bell type) and like the Kleophon Painter, his work is distinguished by purity of line. He is the last of the great artists in the Pheidian tradition, but his work evidences a waning of that influence in a new restlessness. His compositions are less tranquil than those of his master and his figures are plumper, more solid and sensuous, with looser drapery and more use of shading to show depth. His work leads toward the ornateness which became characteristic of late fifth century vase painting. No potters' names or *kalos* names are found on his works, though he occasionally named the characters he was depicting.

Other classicists among the late followers of Polygnotos include the *Chrysis Painter*, the *Kadmos Painter*, the *Pothos Painter* and two whose names are known from *egrapsen* signatures, *Polion* (on a volute-krater, New York 27.122.8) and *Aison* (on a kylix, Madrid 11265). Like the Kleophon Painter and the Dinos Painter, most of these artists preferred Dionysian scenes.

The Exquisite Tradition

The *Meidias Painter* continued the style of the Eretria Painter and developed it into softer more luxurious forms and sometimes into over-sweetness. His compositions depict the female world of the time, particularly in the boudoir and are peopled with women arranging their hair or dress, playing with children or being courted. Effeminate cupids and symbolic figures of Health, Happiness and the like are interspersed in the scenes. Though respectable, the figures are sensual, rather heavy-limbed, mannered and posed affectedly. Their clothing is rich, clinging, usually diaphanous and drawn with a multitude of fine lines which follow each curve of the body. The figures frequently were depicted on several levels. As Arthur Lane remarks "he discarded all the precariously integrated architectures of shape and painted design that earlier potters [and painters] had thought so important."[5] Though Lane goes on to assert that he was happiest "painting small toilet boxes and the like—covering them with plump little trollops in gauze," others regard him as one of the last great figures in Attic vase painting, a celebrated and delicate draftsman and as an artist whose influence carried on well into the fourth century.[6] At the very least, it must be recognized that the several hundred items produced in his style indicate that he had great influence at the time.[7] Beazley credits the Meidias Painter with only twenty-three items, but notes that it is difficult to distinguish his poorer works from those of his many followers.[8] *Aristophanes (egraphe* on kylikes, Berlin 2531 and Boston 00.344 and *egrapsen* on a bell-krater fragment at Agrigento), for example, has been regarded by some authorities as the Meidias Painter in an earlier phase.

The name-piece of the Meidias Painter is a kalpis type hydria (London E 224; see Plate 56), which is signed *Meidias epoiesen* and it is conceivable that potter and painter are one person.[9] Decorated in two tiers, this vase shows the Rape of the Leukippides on the handle zone and Herakles in the Garden of the Hesperides below. Within the upper zone, the figures are shown on different levels suggestive of depth (common to his work and that of his followers) and are foreshortened. On his smaller works, there is sometimes real charm, but his larger works are weakly composed and tend to become ornate with added white and gilded details. He sometimes inscribed the names of characters and he used both *kalos* names (Dikaios and Ganymedes) and *kalé* names (Epicharis and Myrrhinske).

Among his better followers are Aristophanes, mentioned above, who worked with the potter Erginos, the *Nikias Painter* and the *Mikion Painter* (both named after the potters with whom they worked).[10] In addition, there is a group of "sub-Meidian" cup painters, who continued his style.

The Ornate Style

The main trend in vase painting during the late fifth century was toward a highly ornate style on large pots. Compositions were grandiose and crowded with figures placed at varying levels either to fill the whole field or to distinguish the nearer from the farther. Usually, one or two of the figures were painted white with details drawn in yellow-brown dilute. Thick lines of drawing are characteristic as are dark patterns on garments and copious use of white and yellow accessories. Many of the figures, if not most of them, were shown in three-quarter view.

The *Talos Painter* was one of the most successful in the ornate style. He derives his name from his depiction of the death of the bronze giant, Talos, on his only complete remaining work, a volute-krater (Ruvo, Jatta 1501). Painted white and modeled by shading in dilute, the giant is shown falling back into a crowd of spectators all of whom are in orange-red. The figures are shown in different planes one behind the other and the more distant are drawn on a smaller scale. Only a few works have been attributed to this artist—his name-piece, one stand, one loutrophoros and three other pot fragments.

The *Suessula Painter* also must be ranked among the major artists of the period. His name is derived from four neck-amphorae with twisted handles found in a grave at Suessula, near Naples. He is credited with six neck-amphorae and eight kraters. One of these, a neck-amphora at the Metropolitan Museum (New York 17.46.1; see Plate 57) showing a soldier preparing to leave home, is an excellent example of his work. His work is characterized by copious use of white and yellow, richly ornamented garments, lively, restless composition, and violent foreshortening of figures ranged on various levels.

The *Pronomos Painter*, so-called from his depiction of the famous flute player of that name on a volute-krater (Naples 3240, see Plate 58) is credited with only four works, his name-piece, two bell-kraters and one squat lekythos. Despite the paucity of his known works, he is regarded as a major artist. Related to both the Dinos Painter and the Meidias Painter, his style is ornate, with profuse ornamentation and figures arranged in many tiers. His name-piece, showing Pronomos, watched by Dionysos and Ariadne, with a troupe of actors, clearly evidences the influence of the theater on vase painting of this time.[11]

FOURTH CENTURY ATTIC RED-FIGURE ca. 390–320 B.C.

The Attic red-figure vase painting technique was carried over into some of the Greek colonies in southern Italy by immigrant potters and painters. This is evident in some of the early vases produced at the Athenian colony of Thurii (founded ca. 444/3 B.C.) which are difficult to distinguish from products of the homeland.[12] Italian pottery centers also were influenced by Attic styles and, during the years of the Peloponnesian War, the volume of their output increased enormously. By the end of the war, though Attic red-figured works continued to trickle into Magna Graecia to special customers, the vast Italian market was effectively lost to Attic workshops. In the intervening years, new and distinct styles also had been developed in the Italiote centers of Apulia, Campania, Lucania and Paestum as well as in Sicily. Thus, Athenian traders were forced to find new outlets along the northern shores of Africa and, especially, among the Greek colonies in southern Russia.

During the first decades of the fourth century B.C., two relatively distinct styles emerged. Both seem to have been evolved by followers of the Dinos Painter. Some of these followers moved in the direction of crowded, ambitious, florid, highly ornate works, while the others favored simpler, quieter and more refined productions.

Fourth century Attic vase painting appears to have been less well studied than fifth and sixth century work, but a few generalizations may be made. There was more interest in perspective, so that buildings and rectangular objects, when shown, were drawn with receding sides. Lines usually were weaker and thinner. Colors such as white, gold leaf and even pink were sometimes added along with applied clay and figures in relief. The profile eye often was drawn with a very short lower lid[13] and drapery was depicted in flowing lines.[14] Inscriptions of all sorts became very rare; only one potter's signature is known; no painters are known to have signed their works and neither *kalos* nor *kalé* names have been found.

About 470 B.C., the so-called "Kerch" style replaced the ornate and plainer styles. Numerous vases of this type found at Kerch on the Crimean Peninsula of southern Russia (site of ancient Pantikapaion) have given this name to the style. Kerch vases continued in production until about 320 B.C., when they were replaced by the rather poorly decorated or by the impressed and relief work vases of the Hellenistic period.

Barely one thousand vases have been attributed by Beazley[15] as belonging to some 100 plus recognized painters of the fourth century. Of these, almost half are kraters, primarily of the bell type, though there were also many calyx-kraters. Pelikes and lekanides were also fairly important items of production and, during the early decades of the fourth century, stemmed and unstemmed kylikes and skyphoi were common, though later they virtually disappeared as painted items.

The Ornate Style

The most prolific painter of the ornate style is the *Meleager Painter*, named from his depiction of Meleager on at least four works, a volute-krater (Vienna 158), two neck-amphorae (Athens 15113 and Toronto 388) and a calyx-krater (Wurzburg 522). In all, he has 104 attributed works on a variety of shapes from kraters and amphorae to pelikes, kalpides, kylikes, and plates. Most of his scenes are Dionysian, though some come from the palaestra, and are ranged in several tiers on his larger works (see Plate 59 for one of his kalpides, New York 56.171.56).

Perhaps the best exponent of the ornate style is the *Painter of the New York Centauromachy*. He derives his name from a fragmentary volute-krater (New York 06.1021.140; see Plate 60), showing the battle of Lapiths and centaurs at the marriage of Perithoos. His work (of which unfortunately only four fragmentary items are known—two kylikes and a volute-krater, in addition to his name-piece) continues and amplifies upon the work of the Dinos Painter, but is more restless and he employed more additional colors.

The *Xenophantos Painter* derives his name from the only red-figure potter's signature known from the fourth century, *Xenophantos epoiese Athen (aios)* (Xenophantos the Athenian), found on his two attributed works, both squat lekythoi (Leningrad St. 1790 and Leningrad no number). His work closely resembles that of the Meleager Painter. The subjects on both his works are similar, on the body Persians hunting and on the shoulders centauromachies, gigantomachies and Nikai driving chariots. His work is highly ornate with figures partly in relief.

The Plainer Style

The *Jena Painter*, a painter of cups, was quieter and more refined. On his better works, he avoided crowded scenes, attempts at depth or added colors. He drew his heads in profile and gave careful attention to silhouettes with balance of light and dark, being skillful in the use of thin lines to portray graceful figures. He is the last of the great cup painters. His workshop was in Athens, where most of his eighty-one attributed works were found in fragments (almost all kylikes or stemless kylikes).[16] As the majority of these works were taken to Jena, he thus derived his name. Beazley[17] notes that among the works of the Jena Painter's workshop there are some which are clearly by the master himself, some hasty work on the outsides which may be by him, some very careless work which might be his, and other work which is clearly by others.

Exemplifying perhaps best the plainer style is the *Erbach Painter*. His name is derived from a bell-krater at Erbach (no number). He is credited with twelve kraters and one hydria (see Plate 61 for the hydria, New York 56.171.55). These deal with Dionysian subjects in scenes featuring only one or two figures. Several other painters of large items and a number of cup painters also produced uncrowded compositions avoiding the overuse of gilt and other colors and producing calm quiet scenes.

The Kerch Style

The Kerch style resembles that of the Jena Painter in a way, and also appears to derive from that of the Meidias Painter in its polychrome effect, but avoids the latter's clean, sharp outlines, and multitudinous drapery lines (see Plate 62 for an illustration of an early Kerch style kalpis, New York 06.1021.184). At first, composition in this style was simple with flowing lines. By mid-fourth century, however, compositions became crowded, lines sketchy, short, and often harsh in the outlining of body, garments and folds. Hair usually was depicted as wavy strands against a reserved background and profile eyes were shown with a very short lower lid. Subjects were drawn largely from the life of women though often featuring Dionysos, Apollo, Herakles, and Aphrodite and involving erotic subjects or interest in mysticism. Colors were added including white, pink, yellow, gilt, green and blue. Applied clay was often used for relief of figures. Much of the work was cursory, though occasionally a masterpiece is found. Typical of the mature Kerch Style is a chous by the *Pompe Painter* (New York 25.190; see Plate 63) showing the god Dionysos with Pompe. Outstanding artists of the late Kerch Style are the *Marsyas Painter* and the *Mithridates* Painter. One of the better works of the former is a pelike (London 62.5-30-E 424; see Plate 64) showing Pileus taming Thetis. After these artists, the Kerch Style declined and figure painting on vases became obsolete.

SUMMARY

The Kerch style marks the last phase of Attic red-figure vase painting, a technique which had endured for almost two hundred years.

In this chapter, we have seen how the trend toward the ornate, begun in the late fifth century, reached its culmination in the first quarter of the fourth century, gave way briefly to simpler compositions, but then turned once more toward the ornate after the middle of the century with use of more colors and more applied clay until painted pottery finally was replaced by the relief and impressed ware of the Hellenistic period.

Notes on VII—Decline of the Red-figure Technique

1. Beazley, *ARV*, lists about two hundred painters and groups as working in the years ca. 450–420 B.C. and less than one hundred for the years ca. 420-390 B.C. He notes that about twenty-five of the former group are transitional painters and could be considered as late fifth century artists. I have so considered some of them (e.g., the late followers of Polygnotos).

2. Devambez, *Gr. Painting*, p. 29 makes this suggestion.

3. See Appendix II, Figures A17, A35, A38, A55, A69 and A70 for typical depictions of the human body and drapery.

4. At one time, he was called the "Atalante Painter" from his depiction of that mythical princess on a calyx-krater (Bologna 300).

5. Lane, *Greek Pottery*, p. 57.

6. Richter, *Survey*, p. 146, Cook, *Greek P. P.*, p. 184, and Arias and Hirmer, *Greek Vase Painting*, p. 376.

7. Beazley, *ARV*, as amended by *Paralipomena*.

8. Beazley, *ARV*, Chapter 70, pp. 1312 ff., Richter, *Survey*, p. 146-47.

9. Arias and Hirmer, *Greek Vase Painting*, p. 375.

10. The name of the Mikion Painter may, in fact, be Euemporos, as that name has been found on a lekanis (Athens Pnyx P 349) and on a plaque (Athens Acr. 1051), but neither signature is surely identified as that of the painter.

11. For a discussion of the influence of the theater on Attic vase painting, see Webster, *Potter and Patron,* pp. 250-69.

12. Robertson, *Greek Painting,* p. 156.

13. See Appendix II, Figure A36 and A37.

14. Ibid., Figure A71.

15. Beazley, *ARV,* and *Paralipomena.*

16. Another cup painter, the Diomed Painter, with three attributed works, may, in fact, be identical with the Jena Painter.

17. *ARV,* Vol. II, Chapter 89.

VIII

Retrospect

As we have seen, Attic red-figure was born out of a reversal of the color scheme of the black-figure technique. It flowered during a period of some fifty years, from about 520 to about 470 B.C. Thereafter, it slowly lost its strength and appeal.

During the two hundred years of its existence, the technique was influenced by various factors. First, of course, was the tradition of the older black-figure technique. Next, came the aristocratic youth of Athens, whose influence moved it in the direction of portrayal of everyday life in place of mythology. The victories of Marathon and Salamis brought new exuberance and joy to the vase painters' output. Mural art and classic sculpture of the Periclean Age led vase painters to emulate these art forms and to tone down depictions of the old myths. A bit later, the emancipation of women resulted in effeminate and exquisite compositions. The Athenian plague and defeat in the Peloponnesian War were reflected in vase painting by heaviness and melancholy scenes. Loss of the vast Italian (especially Etruscan) markets reinforced a trend toward ornateness, since this style appealed to the new barbarian markets along the Black Sea littoral.

Perhaps, however, reason for decline of the red-figure technique lies deeper than any of these influences. While we know little about painting on walls and on fabrics during the Archaic period, they appear not to have been of major importance. Apparently, it was vase painting which attracted the better artists of the time. Appearance of Polygnotos of Thasos and Nikon of Athens in the 460s B.C. seems to have marked the real beginning of mural painting as a major new field of art. Unquestionably, many artists who might otherwise have done vase painting turned to the new form. Similarly, they must have been attracted into architecture, sculpture, and bas-relief, as Athens was rebuilt after the Persian War. Finally, perhaps most important of all, is the fact that the possibilities for development of the red-figure technique had been almost exhausted by Archaic artists.

By the second quarter of the fifth century, little remained to be done, except for a few refinements such as development of a true profile eye. As we have seen, some artists continued in red-figure, while others tried white-ground work. Many, however, must have simply turned to other fields of art. The success or failure of those who remained depended on the individual genius of the artist so that some very fine red-figure work continued to be produced well after the technique itself had passed its zenith. With such exceptions, the red-figure technique slowly declined. By 320 B.C., pottery was simply painted black or decorated with festoons of ivy or laurel, wreaths, vines, checquers and the like or was provided with molded or impressed designs.

Summary Chart
and
Appendixes

SUMMARY CHART
(Dates approximate)

MAJOR PERIODS	STYLISTIC AND OTHER DEVELOPMENTS	MAJOR PAINTERS	MAJOR POTTERS	PREVALENT SHAPES	PERIOD OF POPULARITY IN RED-FIGURE
EARLY ARCHAIC ca. 530-500 B.C.	Invention of the red-figure technique. Changes to old black-figure conventions: Abandonment of incision. Reduction in use of colors. Attempts to portray body and drapery more naturally. Everyday life scenes begin to appear along side of mythological scenes.	Andokides P. Psiax Phintias Euthymides Euphronios Oltos Epiktetos Smikros Sosias P.	Andokides* Nikosthenes** Pamphaios* Hischylos* Charinos* Chelis* Euergides* Kachrylion* Paidikos* Euxitheos*	Type A kylix** Type B kylix Type A amphora** Type B amphora** Type C amphora** Calyx-krater** Type A neck-amphora** Stamnos Kalpis Stemless kylix**	ca. 530-500 B.C. ca. 525-4th Century B.C. ca. 530-450 B.C. ca. 530-425 B.C. ca. 530-470 B.C. ca. 530 throughout red-figure ca. 530-400 and to 420 B.C. ca. 530-450 and to 420 B.C. ca. 530-400 B.C. ca. 530-350 B.C.
	Emphasis on portrayal of strength, muscles, bones, and complicated poses. Kalos names (but no kalē names).	Hypsis Skythes Euergides P.	Tleson	Phiale** Skyphos** Pelike	ca. 530-350 B.C. ca. 500-350 B.C. ca. 500-400 B.C.
			Pistoxenos* Python	Type B neck-amphora** Volute-krater**	Scattered 530 B.C. and after
LATE ARCHAIC ca. 500-475 B.C.	Refinement of red-figure: its apogee. Progress in portrayal of human body and drapery.	Berlin P. Kleophrades P.	Kleophrades	Oinochoe** All above vase shapes (except Type A kylix) plus Nolan amphora.	ca. 500-400 B.C.
	Gradual abandonment of panel compositions, introduction of "Spotlight" compositions, changes in composition on cups. Emphasis on grace of pose and expression of mood in rhythmic patterns. Appearance of kalē names.	Onesimos Brygos P. Makron Douris Nikoxenos P. Eucharides P. Antiphon P. Colmar P. Foundry P. Myson	Euphronios* Brygos* Hieron* Douris	Bell-krater Type C kylix Squat lekythos Pointed amphora	ca. 490-400 B.C. ca. 490-400 B.C. ca. 490-460 B.C. ca. 500-400 B.C. ca. 500-400 B.C.

164

MAJOR PERIODS	STYLISTIC AND OTHER DEVELOPMENTS	MAJOR PAINTERS	MAJOR POTTERS	PREVALENT SHAPES	PERIOD OF POPULARITY IN RED-FIGURE
EARLY CLASSICAL FREE STYLE ca. 475-450 B.C.	Dilemma of the red-figure technique: after its apogee. Development of mural art as a competitor and as an influence. Traditionalism: the mannerists. Inspiration from mural painting. Pre-classicism. Naturalism. Emphasis on expression of emotion through facial expression, gesture or posture and portrayal of a uniform concept of human beauty and dignity; daily life emphasized more than mythology. Both *kalos* and *kalē* names employed. Classical eye replaced Archaic eye. Beginnings of white-ground work.	Pan P. Niobid P. Villa Giulia P. Penthesileia P. Pistoxenos P. Hermonax Sabouroff P. Pig P. Altamura P. Blenheim P. Methyse P. Chicago P. Sotades P. Tymbos P.	Sotades* Megakles Euphronios (see above) Pistoxenos (see above)	Above vase shapes (except Type A neck-amphora) plus Loutrophoros.** Column-krater** Shoulder lekythos**	ca. 470-420 B.C. ca. 475-425 B.C. ca. 475-400 B.C.
CLASSICAL FREE STYLE ca. 450-420 B.C.	Periclean beautification of Athens by master sculptors, architects and muralists. Trends in vase painting: Archaism: the mannerists. Inspiration from murals and sculpture. Classicism. Exquisiteness. Flowering of white-ground work. Emphasis on portrayal of idealized human beauty and dignity in serene scenes. Both *kalos* and *kalē* names employed.	Nausikaa P. Polygnotos Achilles P. Eretria P. White-ground specialists.	Epigenes	Above vase shapes (except Type A amphora and Type C kylix). Period of great popularity of the shoulder lekythos in white-ground.	

MAJOR PERIODS	STYLISTIC AND OTHER DEVELOPMENTS	MAJOR PAINTERS	MAJOR POTTERS	PREVALENT SHAPES	PERIOD OF POPULARITY IN RED-FIGURE
LATE 5th CENTURY ca. 420-390 B.C.	Reduction in output due to the Peloponnesian War: loss of markets. Mood of painting sad and melancholy or reflective of boudoir and life of women. Classic tradition. Exquisite tradition. Ornate style. Decline and end of white-ground work. Trend in vase painting toward increasing ornateness. Kalos and kalé names few.	Kleophon P. Dinos P. Meidias P. Talos P. Suessula P. Pronomos P. Aristophanes	Meidias Erginos	Most of above vase shapes (except Type B amphora, pointed amphora, pelike, stamnos, column-krater and loutrophoros), but in greatly reduced numbers. Last of shoulder lekythos about 400 B.C.	
FOURTH CENTURY ca. 490-320 B.C.	Loss of Italian markets; new markets along the Black Sea shores. General trend in vase painting and potting toward ornateness. Plainer style. Ornate style. "Kerch" style. Interest in perspective, much use of added colors and applied clay. Inscriptions rare; no kalos or kalé names, no painters' signatures, only one potters' name known.	Meleager P. P. of N.Y. Centauromachy Xenophantos P. Jena P. Erbach P. Marsyas P. Mithridates P.	Xenophantos	Painted shapes included some amphora shapes. The kalpis, calyx- and bell-kraters. Type B kylikes, skyphoi, phialai, and stemless kylikes with a few other shapes.	

*Potted five or more works with signatures.
**Previously done in black-figure.

APPENDIX I

NOTES ON ATTRIBUTIONS

The fact that I have credited a particular number of items to any one painter does not, of course, mean that this is all the work he ever did. For any given artist there are many works which have not been found. The number given is that shown for the artist by Sir John Davidson Beazley in his *Attic Red-figure Vase Painters* (as amended by his *Paralipomena*). Other authorities have attributed additional works to various artists; Beazley has accepted some of these attributions, but not others. For the purposes of this book, it has appeared best to employ those given or accepted by Beazley.

Beazley was extremely careful to differentiate as among vases painted by a painter, in his manner, in imitation of his work, by his followers, in his workshop, school, circle, or group, under his influence or akin to his work. I have maintained clear distinctions between items actually by a painter and those otherwise related to him. Thus, I have included reference to works in a painter's manner only if they appear to be very close to the painter's own work. Serious students should refer to Beazley's works for these distinctions.

Finally, it should be noted that attributed items are not necessarily complete items. If the shape of a fragment permits identification of the original shape, it is so listed; thus, an identifiable cup fragment is listed as a cup.

APPENDIX II

STYLISTIC DEVELOPMENTS

This appendix is based on personal observation supplemented by reading—in particular, Miss Gisela M. A. Richter's *Attic Red-figured Vases: A Survey* and R. M. Cook's *Greek Painted Pottery*. While acknowledging my debt to both these eminent scholars, I wish to accept responsibility for errors of interpretation or of observation. Furthermore, it should be noted that while statements made as to characteristic styles of any given period should be accepted as generally true, there were always exceptions. In a few cases, I have indicated or illustrated exceptions, but generally I have ignored them as unnecessarily confusing to the coherency of the normal trend of developments.

In the text, changes in portrayal of the various features of the human body were summarized in discussion of the stages of development of the red-figure technique. This appendix enables the reader to follow the evolution of these features (head, hair, eyes, musculature of the torso—as well as of drapery) from ca. 530 B.C. to the fourth century B.C. with illustrations. Other features of vase painting (subsidiary ornamentation, framing of pictures, and colors used) are also discussed briefly.

I. The Human Body

Head and Hair

Early Archaic Red-figure Style ca. 530–500 B.C.

Certain conventions were carried over from the black-figure technique into red-figure. Thus, in general, a profile head with a frontal eye was normal and the chin line usually stopped abruptly where it met the neck line. Hair was drawn as a black mass with curls or short strands at the brow, temple, and neck. At first, incision was employed to outline hair and beards and to indicate individual locks (Figs. A1 and A2). Gradually, reserving replaced incision for these features (Fig. A3 illustrates this transition, showing the hair outlined by incision, but with the beard reserved against the black background). Soon, incision was abandoned in favor of reserving (Figs. A4 and A5). There were, however, exceptions to these rules (Fig. A6 shows a head with long locks at the temple and neck in combination with incision, while Fig. A7 illustrates a rare frontal face).

Fig. A1 *(after the Andokides Painter)*

Fig. A2 *(after Phintias)*

Fig. A3 *(after Euthymides)*

Fig. A4 *(after Oltos)*

Fig. A5 *(after Oltos)*

Fig. A6 *(after the Andokides Painter)*

Fig. A7 (after Phintias)

Late Archaic Style ca. 500–475 B.C.

The head continued to be drawn normally in profile. Hair was still drawn as a solid black mass with dots or short strands at the forehead; often, however, long curling locks were added behind (Figs. A8 and A9—longer strands in front). Sometimes hair was drawn with solid straight or wavy lines against a dilute background (Figs. A10 and A11) and there was a tendency for hair to flow with the motion of the body. Incision was virtually abandoned and the chin line was frequently continued beyond the neck line to mark the contour of the jaw (Figs. A10 and A11).

Fig. A8 (after the Kleophrades Painter)

Fig. A9 (after the Berlin Painter)

Fig. A11 (after the Brygos
Painter)

Fig. A10 (after the Berlin
Painter)

Early Classical Free Style ca. 475–450 B.C.

Though rendering of the three-quarter view of the face was mastered and appeared relatively frequently, the profile head continued to be the most prevalent with the jaw line clearly indicated. Hair was variously depicted. Usually it was shown as a black mass with a wavy contour over the brow and temples (Fig. A12) or with curls at brow and temple (Fig. A13) and as a black mass in back. More often than previously, hair was drawn as separate strands against a dilute background or even directly on the orange-red background (Fig. A14—on white-ground work).

Fig. A12 (after Hermonax)

Fig. A13 (after the Penthesileia
Painter)

171

Fig. A14 (after the White-
ground Pistoxenos Painter)

Classical Free Style and After: ca. 450–Fourth Century.

By mid-fifth century, drawing of the head and hair had been fully mastered; variations thereafter appear to be the result of whims of the individual artists (Figs. A15 and A16). Frontal and three-quarter views of the head were done with ease, though the profile head always remained the favorite. Hair was depicted in various ways—often as a loose mass of wavy contours at the forehead and temples and as fluffy curls at the side. With the passage of time, hair generally was indicated by separate strands drawn against a reserved background (Fig. A17 is from a white-ground work).

Fig. A15 (after the Achilles Painter)

Fig. A16 (after the Kleophon Painter)

Fig. A17 (after Group R)
White-ground

Eye

Early Archaic Red-figure Style ca. 530–500 B.C.

In the black-figure technique, the male eye was incised and very rounded (Fig. A18), while the female eye had been painted against white flesh and was elongated (Fig. A19). In early red-figured works the eye continued to be drawn as a frontal eye, but the old distinction between the male eye and the female eye was quickly abandoned. At first, the eye was drawn with wide curves and with a black dot or a circle and a dot for the iris (Figs. A20 and A21) and the male eye was drawn more rounded than the female eye. Soon, however, the eye was drawn with two simple shallow curves meeting at both corners (Fig. A22) and the distinction between male and female eye was eliminated. Later, the curves depicting the eye became asymmetrical to indicate the difference between the outer corner of the eye and the inner corner with its tear duct (Figs. A23–A25). During this early period, portrayal of eyelashes was relatively common on more elaborate works. Later, eyelashes were more often omitted.

Fig. A18 (after the Lysippides Painter)

Fig. A19 (after Psiax)

Fig. A20 (after the Andokides Painter)

Fig. A21 (after the Andokides Painter)

Fig. A22 (after the Andokides
Painter)

Fig. A23 (after Phintias)

Fig. A24 (after Euphronios)

Fig. A25 (after Euphronios)

Late Archaic Style ca. 500–475 B.C.

In the late Archaic period, though the eye continued to be shown frontally in a profile face, the iris was moved towards the nose and the inner end of the eye was left open to suggest a profile view. The iris continued to be depicted as a circle with a dot or as a large black dot, while lashes were added at the whim of the painter. Gradually, attempts were made to express emotion through the eyes. (Figs. A26–A28 show typical eyes of this period.)

Fig. A26 (after the Kleophrades
Painter)

Fig. A27 (after the Berlin
Painter)

Fig. A28 (after the Berlin
Painter)

Early Classical Free Style ca. 475–450 B.C.

One of the distinguishing features of the Classical style of the red-figure technique is the change from the frontal eye (often called the "Archaic eye") in a profile face to a developed profile eye. At first, while the outline of the eye was drawn as an acute angle of two curving lines and, thus was clearly in profile, the

174

iris continued to be shown frontally as a circle with a dot or as a single large black dot (Figs. A29-A31). The iris, however, was placed at the front of the open eye. The upper line of the eye was either extended beyond the lower line or was branched to indicate lashes. Sometimes two lines were used to indicate the upper lid (Fig. A31). Increasingly, emotion was conveyed by the eye.

Frontal or three-quarter faces usually were drawn with both eyes shown in profile so that the result appeared cross-eyed or as squinting. Sometimes, however, both corners were closed and the iris placed convincingly in the center.

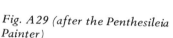

Fig. A29 (after the Penthesileia Painter)

Fig. A30 (after the Niobid Painter)

Fig. A31 (after Hermonax)

Classical Free Style ca. 450–420 B.C.

As the Classical period progressed, the triangular profile eye became the norm. Depiction of the iris, however, continued to develop. Drawn less round and more elongated, it tended to touch only the upper lid, while the pupil was usually omitted. Soon, the iris was drawn as a solid black curved triangle, thus appearing realistically in profile (Figs. A32–A33).

The upper lid usually was drawn with two curved lines and with one or more curves added for lashes.

The eyes in frontal or three-quarter faces were rendered with both the inner and outer corners closed or with both corners open; the iris was centered in either case (Fig. A34).

Fig. A32 (after the Achilles Painter)

Fig. A33 (after the Kleophon Painter)

Fig. A34 (after the Peleus Painter)

175

Late Fifth Century and Fourth Century Styles

In general, after the Classical eye was fully developed, there was little change in its depiction. In the late fifth century, the lower lid tended to be drawn a little shorter than previously (Fig. A35), and in the fourth century, it frequently was drawn with a very short line (Fig. A36).

The frontal eye usually was drawn with both inner and outer corners open and with the iris convincingly located (Figs. A37 and A38).

Fig. A35 (after the Dinos Painter)

Fig. A36 (after the Marsyas Painter)

Fig. A37 (after the Meleager Painter)

Fig. A38 (after Group R) White-ground

Body and Legs

Early Archaic Red-figure Style ca. 530–500 B.C.

In the black-figure technique, the human body had been portrayed as a composite of its component parts: head, normally in profile, a frontal trunk and legs in profile. At first, red-figure artists took over this contorted portrayal, but soon they began to attempt to show the human body in more natural poses. Freed from the strictures imposed by incision, they began to show bone structure and muscles in movement, employing black and dilute lines. Black relief lines usually were used to indicate bones such as the collar bones, shoulder blades, hips, spine and ankles, while muscles were usually indicated by dilute lines. Soon attempts were made to show torsion by drawing collar bones of unequal length (Fig. A39) and by drawing a frontal body with one leg in profile (Fig. A40). Gradually, great advances were made toward rendering a three-quarter view of the torso (Figs. A41 and A42). Profile views seem to have been less successful (Fig. A43).

The female form appears to have presented difficulties for early red-figure artists (Figs. A44 and A45). Thus, in a frontal body, breasts were drawn as two profiles, while in a side view usually only one breast was shown, or if two were indicated, one was above the other. Interest in muscles, so evident in portrayal of male bodies, was lacking in rendering the female form and it became conventional not to portray muscles for women.

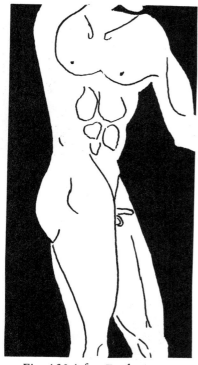

Fig. A39 (after Euphronios)

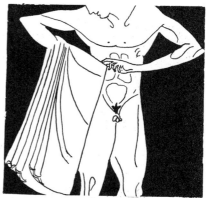

Fig. A40 (after Euphronios)

Fig. A42 (after Euthymides)

Fig. A41 (after Euthymides)

Fig. A43 (after Phintias)

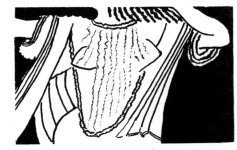

Fig. A44 (after Euphronios)

Fig. A45 (after Oltos)

Late Archaic Style ca. 500–475 B.C.

As the three-quarter view was mastered gradually, the full profile body became increasingly rare. When so drawn, the chest was contracted on the farther side and often a curve was added to show part of the farther shoulder (Fig. A46). In the increasingly more common three-quarter view, collar bones were either contracted on the farther side or omitted, stomach muscles were contracted on the farther side to show torsion and legs were drawn one in profile and the other full front, full back, or even in three-quarter view (Fig. A47). In general, muscles were indicated increasingly by dilute lines.

Females seldom were drawn either full front or in full profile, since, though not fully mastered, the three-quarter view was becoming increasingly satisfactory (Fig. A48). Female breasts, which had given earlier artists so much trouble, were drawn side by side in profile both pointing in the same direction or one was drawn full front and the other in profile (Figs. A49 and A51).

Fig. A46 (after the Berlin Painter)

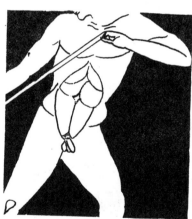

Fig. A47 (after the Kleophrades Painter)

Fig. A48 (after the Kleophrades Painter)

Fig. A49 (after Onesimos)

Fig. A51 (after Douris)

Fig. A50 (after Onesimos)

Early Classical Free Style ca. 475–450 B.C.

During the quarter century preceding 450 B.C. drawing of three-quarter views of both male and female bodies was fully mastered with the farther sides convincingly forshortened (Figs. A52–A54). Even legs were successfully drawn in three-quarter views, though frequently the ankle was misplaced. Shading came more into use to show roundness of form.

Fig. A52 (after the Euaion Painter)

Fig. A53 (after the Pan Painter)

180

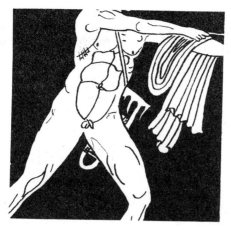

Fig. A54 (after the Niobid Painter)

Classical Free Style and After: ca. 450–Fourth Century B.C.

Despite complete mastery of the three-quarter view of the human body, profile and to a lesser extent frontal views continued to predominate. Shading came to be used more to show bones, muscles, and roundness of form. Gradually, women came to predominate in the scenes and male figures tended to become increasingly effeminate (Fig. A55).

Fig. A55 (after the Meidias Painter)

II. DRAPERY

Early Archaic Red-figure Style ca. 530–500 B.C.

In the very earliest red-figure work drapery was flat, falling straight and shadowless. At first, the lower edges were drawn with zigzags running only in one direction (Fig. A56). Later, pleats became elaborate with zigzags at the bottom running in the two directions from a central pleat (Fig. A57). Groups of pleats often were separated by smooth unpleated areas (Fig. A58). Throughout this period, the farther edge of the chiton was indicated by a wavy or curving line (Figs. A56–A58). The himation (or mantle) was drawn in the same way, but with larger pleats (Fig. A57).

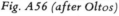

Fig. A56 (after Oltos)

Fig. A57 (after Smikros)

Fig. A58 (after Euthymides)

Ripe Archaic Style ca. 500–475 B.C.

In the quarter century after 500 B.C., artists drew the central pleat of the chiton narrower and less high than previously and the groups of pleats closer together (Fig. A59). A little later, the zigzags became less regular and the pleats no longer were arranged in groups. More important, at this point, the lines of the folds often were curved to follow the action of the figures (Figs. A60-A62). Still later, the zigzags tended to disappear and the lower edge of the chiton was drawn as a wavy line, as a series of arcs or as one curving line. The himation was at first drawn with more or less pointed zigzags and the folds as straight radiating lines (Fig. A59). Later, the zigzags of the himation became more rounded and the folds more diversified (Fig. A61).

182

Fig. A59 (after Douris)

Fig. A60 (after the Berlin Painter)

Fig. A61 (after the Kleophrades Painter)

Fig. A62 (after Douris)

Early Classical Free Style ca. 475–450 B.C.

By the beginning of the Classical period, drapery was assuming natural shapes and had depth (Figs. A63–A66). The farther edge of chiton or himation was seldom indicated (Figs. A64 and A66). The peplos (which had been out of fashion since about 530 B.C. but came back into style again) was rendered by a few lines to indicate the heavy folds and often had bold rounded zigzags along the edge. The himation was similarly drawn with a few lines and zigzags along the edges.

Fig. A63 (after the Oreithyia
Painter)

Fig. A64 (after the Pistoxenos
Painter)

Fig. A65 (after the Niobid
Painter)

184

Fig. A66 (after the Niobid
Painter)

Classical Free Style ca. 450–420 B.C.

By mid-fifth century, drapery was normally drawn in flowing lines, varying in direction to indicate motion and the round forms of the body beneath (Figs. A67–A68). Thinned washes often were employed to indicate shadows and depths of folds.

Fig. A67 (after the Phiale Painter)

Fig. A68 (after the Kleophon Painter)

Late Fifth Century Century Style ca. 420–390 B.C.

Drapery became rich, thin, and clinging with multitudinous folds following the contours of the limbs and bodies (Figs. A69–A70) or flowing as in Figure 68 above.

Fig. A69 (after the Meidias Painter)

Fig. A70 (after the Pronomos Painter)

Fourth Century Style

By mid-fourth century, drapery was rendered by many short very thin lines to indicate the actual structure of folds and the shape of the body (Fig. A71).

Fig. A71 (after the Marsyas Painter)

III. SUBSIDIARY ORNAMENTATION

Throughout the period of the red-figure technique, subsidiary ornamentation was generally limited to a few items: meanders, palmettes, tongues, eggs, lotus, ivy, laurel, scrolls, rays, spirals, crosses, chequers, dots, and simple lines, used in a variety of ways, singly or in multiple groupings.

Early Archaic Red-figure Style ca. 530–500 B.C.

Subsidiary ornamentation employed by early red-figure artists was largely inherited from the black-figure technique except for the palmette which (enclosed or free) was large enough to be drawn in outline. Black-figure relics included the single and doubled chain of lotus and palmettes, tongues, eggs, ivy, base rays, etc.

Late Archaic Style ca. 500–475 B.C.

Some old black-figure ornaments were still retained. Base rays, however, were abandoned along with handle vines. The simple meander was often employed (frequently with interruptions of squares containing crosses). A delicate palmette was sometimes set obliquely in a band. In general, subsidiary ornamentation played a smaller role than either earlier or later.

Early Classical Style ca. 475–450 B.C.

Old black-figure patterns remained in some use, but the lotus and palmette were contorted into elaborate and novel shapes and were often used alone. Generally the trend was towards profuse and rather straggly growth.

Classical Free Style ca. 450–420 B.C.

Subsidiary ornamentation underwent little change except for a greater tendency towards abstract elasticity.

Late Fifth Century Style ca. 420–390 B.C.

Subsidiary ornamentation became rather discreet.

Fourth Century Style

There was little change in subsidiary ornamentation though the palmette was trimmed down almost beyond recognition to a low triangle. Bands of spiral hooks became common.

IV. FRAMING OF PICTURES

Early Archaic Red-figure Style ca. 530–500 B.C.

The tondos of cups were not surrounded by any band of ornament. Palmettes were usual at cup handles. Amphorae usually had the picture framed by a panel. On other large pots palmettes usually served as frames for the picture.

Late Archaic Style and After: ca. 500–475 B.C.

Cup tondos usually were framed by a band of meander; palmettes, however, were often omitted at the handles. Panels were abandoned on amphorae and other pots and figures stood on a strip of ornament or were left in the air. By ca. 450 B.C., figures either were ranged on a base line running around the entire pot or were placed on different levels; in either case, they tended to fill the entire painted area.

V. COLORS

The red-figure technique is essentially two color in contrast to the black-figure technique which employed reds and white liberally in addition to the black of the silhouette and the orange-red of the background. White previously used in the black-figure technique for the flesh of women was abandoned at once and elsewhere white was seldom used, except occasionally, for the hair of old men. The various shades of red ranging to purple were also restricted in use primarily to wreathes, fillets and inscriptions. As the Archaic period progressed, purple was employed even less, and dilute brown was substituted for accessories. In the early Classical period occasional touches of red were applied over white; gilded clay, red-brown and purple-brown also appeared rarely. Use of red over white and gilding came into fairly common use in the free Classical style after mid-fifth century. By the late fifth century B.C., the red-figure technique had passed its prime; white, yellow and gold became common in an ornate style and in the fourth century, white, pink and gold plus occasional blue and green all appeared as added colors.

FIGURES IN APPENDIX II

A1. From the amphora F 2159 by the Andokides Painter in Berlin (Redrawn from Arias and Hirmer, *A History of Greek Vase Painting*— cited hereafter as Arias and Hirmer—Plate 83).

A2. From the amphora RC 6843 by Phintias in Tarquinia (Redrawn from Arias and Hirmer, Plate 93).

A3. From the amphora 2307 by Euthymides in Munich (Redrawn from Arias and Hirmer, Plate 117).

A4. From the kylix RC 6848 by Oltos in Tarquinia (Redrawn from Arias and Hirmer, Plate 104).

A5. From the same kylix (Redrawn from Arias and Hirmer, Plate 102).

A6. From the amphora F 2159 by the Andokides Painter in Berlin (Redrawn from Arias and Hirmer, Plate 83).

A7. From the amphora 6843 by Phintias in Tarquinia (Redrawn from Arias and Hirmer, Plate 95).

A8. From the pointed amphora 2344 by the Kleophrades Painter in Munich (Redrawn from Arias and Hirmer, Plate XXX).

A9. From the Amphora F 2160 by the Berlin Painter in Berlin (Redrawn from Arias and Hirmer, Plate 153).

A10. From the same amphora (Redrawn from Arias and Hirmer, Plate 152).

A11. From the kylix G 152 by the Brygos Painter in the Louvre (Redrawn from Arias and Hirmer, Plate 141).

A12. From the stamnos 2413 by Hermonax in Munich (Redrawn from Arias and Hirmer, Plate 182).

A13. From the kylix 2689 by the Penthesileia Painter in Munich (Redrawn from Arias and Hirmer, Plate 171).

A14. From the kylix by the Pistoxenos Painter in Taranto (Redrawn from Arias and Hirmer, Plate 167).

A15. From the amphora by the Achilles Painter in the Vatican (Redrawn from Arias and Hirmer, Plate XL).

A16. From the stamnos 2415 by the Kleophon Painter in Munich (Redrawn from Arias and Hirmer, Plate 194).

A17. From the lekythos 1816 by Group R in Athens (Redrawn from Arias and Hirmer, Plate XLV).

A18. From the hydria B 302 by the Lysippides Painter in London (Redrawn from Arias and Hirmer, Plate 69).

A19. From the amphora by Psiax in Brescia (Redrawn from Arias and Hirmer, Plate XX).

A20. From the amphora F 2169 by the Andokides Painter in Berlin (Redrawn from Arias and Hirmer, Plate 83).

A21. From the same amphora (Redrawn from Arias and Hirmer, Plate 83).

A22. From the same amphora (Redrawn from Arias and Hirmer, Plate 86).

A23. From the amphora RC 6843 by Phintias in Tarquinia (Redrawn from Arias and Hirmer, Plate 93).

A24. From the calyx-krater F 2180 by Euphronios in Berlin (Redrawn from Arias and Hirmer, Plate 112).

A25. From the volute-krater 1465 by Euphronios in Arezzo (Redrawn from Arias and Hirmer, Plate 115).

A26. From the pointed amphora 2344 by the Kleophrades Painter in Munich (Redrawn from Arias and Hirmer, Plate 123).

A27. From the Nolan amphora III.I.40 by the Berlin Painter in Manchester (Redrawn from Cook, R.M., *Greek Painted Pottery*, Plate 37A).

A28. From the amphora F 2160 by the Berlin Painter in Berlin (Redrawn from Arias and Hirmer, Plate 152).

A29. From the kylix 2689 by the Penthesileia Painter in Munich (Redrawn from Arias and Hirmer, Plate 171).

A30. From the calyx-krater MNC 511 (G 341) by the Niobid Painter in the Louvre (Redrawn from Arias and Hirmer, Plate 175).

A31. From the stamnos 2413 by Hermonax in Munich (Redrawn from Arias and Hirmer, Plate 182).

A32. From the amphora by the Achilles Painter in the Vatican (Redrawn from Arias and Hirmer, Plate XL).

A33. From the stamnos 2415 by the Kleophon Painter in Munich (Redrawn from Arias and Hirmer, Plate 194).

A34. From the amphora 47.9-9.7 (E 271) by the Peleus Painter in London (Redrawn from Cook, R.M., *Greek P.P.*, Plate 46A).

A35. From the stamnos 2419 by the Dinos Painter in Naples (Redrawn from Arias and Hirmer, Plate 211).

A36. From the pelike E 424 by the Marsyas Painter in London (Redrawn from Arias and Hirmer, Plate XLVII).

A37. From the stemless cup E 129 by the Meleager Painter in London (Redrawn from Arias and Hirmer, Plate 222).

A38. From the lekythos 1816 by Group R in Athens (Redrawn from Arias and Hirmer, Plate XLV).

A39. From the calyx-krater F 2180 by Euphronios in Berlin (Redrawn from Arias and Hirmer, Plate 112).

A40. From the same calyx-krater (Redrawn from Arias and Hirmer, Plate 112).

A41. From the amphora 2307 by Euthymides in Munich (Redrawn from Arias and Hirmer, Plate 117).

A42. From the same amphora (Redrawn from Arias and Hirmer, Plate 117).

A43. From the amphora G 42 by Phintias in the Louvre (Redrawn from Arias and Hirmer, Plate 91).

A44. From the calyx-krater G 103 by Euphronios in the Louvre (Redrawn from Arias and Hirmer, Plate 111).

A45. From the kylix RC 6848 by Oltos in Tarquinia (Redrawn from Arias and Hirmer, Plate 103).

A46. From the amphora F 2160 by the Berlin Painter in Berlin (Redrawn from Arias and Hirmer, Plate 150).

A47. From the calyx-krater RC 4196 by the Kleophrades Painter in Tarquinia (Redrawn from Arias and Hirmer, Plate 119).

A48. From the hydria 2422 by the Kleophrades Painter in Naples (Redrawn from Arias and Hirmer, Plate 125).

A49. From the kylix fragment 30.1 by Onesimos at Bowdoin College (Redrawn from Cook, R.M., *Greek P.P.*, Plate 40).

A50. From the kylix A 889 by Onesimos in Brussels (Redrawn from Arias and Hirmer, Plate 149).

A51. From the kylix 23.160.54 by Douris in New York (Redrawn from Richter, G.M.A., *Attic Red-figured Vases: A Survey*, Fig. 65).

A52. From the kylix 06.1021.177 by the Euaion Painter in New York (Redrawn from Richter, *Survey*, Fig. 87).

A53. From the bell-krater V 778 by the Pan Painter in Palermo (Redrawn from Arias and Hirmer, Plate 161).

A54. From the calyx-krater MNC 511 (G 341) by the Niobid Painter in the Louvre (Redrawn from Arias and Hirmer, Plate 175).

A55. From the hydria 81947 by the Meidias Painter in Florence (Redrawn from Arias and Hirmer, Plate 217).

A56. From the Nikosthenic amphora G 2 by Oltos in the Louvre (Redrawn from Arias and Hirmer, Plate 99).

A57. From the stamnos A 717 by Smikros in Brussels (Redrawn from Arias and Hirmer, Plate 106).

A58. From the amphora 2309 by Euthymides in Munich (Redrawn from Arias and Hirmer, Plate 116).

A59. From the kylix G 115 by Douris in the Louvre (Redrawn from Arias and Hirmer, Plate 144).

A60. From the bell-krater G 175 by the Berlin Painter in the Louvre (Redrawn from Arias and Hirmer, Plate 156).

A61. From the loutrophoros CA 435 by the Kleophrades Painter in the Louvre (Redrawn from Arias and Hirmer, Plate 127).

A62. From the kylix G 104 by Douris in the Louvre (Redrawn from Arias and Hirmer, Plate 148).

A63. From the pointed amphora 2345 by the Oreithyia Painter in Munich (Redrawn from Arias and Hirmer, Plate 159).

A64. From the skyphos 708 by the Pistoxenos Painter in Schwerin (Redrawn from Arias and Hirmer, Plate 166).

A65. From the volute-krater G 1283 by the Niobid Painter in Palermo (Redrawn from Arias and Hirmer, Plate 180).

A66. From the calyx-krater MNC 511 (G 341) by the Niobid Painter in the Louvre (Redrawn from Arias and Hirmer, Plate 175).

A67. From the Nolan amphora 738-1864 by the Phiale Painter in the Victoria and Albert Museum (Redrawn from Lane, Arthur, *Greek Pottery*, Plate 80).

A68. From the pelike 2361 by the Kleophon Painter in Munich (Redrawn from Arias and Hirmer, Plate 197).

A69. From the hydria 81947 by the Meidias Painter in Florence (Redrawn from Arias and Hirmer, Plate XLVI).

A70. From the volute-krater 3240 by the Pronomos Painter in Naples (Redrawn from Arias and Hirmer, Plate 219).

A71. From the nuptial lebes 15592 by the Marsyas Painter in Leningrad (Redrawn from Arias and Hirmer, Plate 228).

APPENDIX III

POTTERS OF RED-FIGURED VASES

For the names of potters of red-figured vases who signed their works, I am indebted to Sir John D. Beazley's *Attic Red-figure Vase Painters*, Appendix II (as amended by his *Paralipomena*). For fragmentary signatures, which I have not included, see his Appendix III.

In presenting this list, it should be noted that the practice of signing was not consistent and not practiced by all potters. Many of the best craftsmen never signed their works at all. Others signed only sporadically and might sign an indifferent piece or fail to sign a masterpiece (in this connection see J. V. Noble, *The Techniques of Attic Painted Pottery*, p. xii).

RED-FIGURE POTTERS

POTTER'S NAME	ASSOCIATION	ITEMS
Agathon	Agathon Painter	1 pyxis
Andokides*	Andokides Painter	4 amphorae and 1 kylix
	Psiax	1 amphora
	Epiktetos	1 calyx-krater
Atitas	Pasiades Painter	1 alabastron
Brygos	Brygos Painter	5 kylikes
	Briseis Painter	2 kylikes
	Painter of Oxford Brygos	1 kylix
	near Castelgiorgio Painter	1 kylix
	Unattributed	6 kylikes
Charinos*	Unattributed	2 mugs, 4 oinochoai, 1 head vase and 1 mug (?)
Chelis	Chelis Painter	1 kylix
	Oltos and Chelis Painter	1 kylix
	Oltos (?) and Thalia Painter	1 kylix
	Euergides Painter	1 kylix
	Oltos	1 kylix

POTTER'S NAME	ASSOCIATION	ITEMS
Deiniades	Phintias	1 kylix
Douris	Douris	1 kantharos and
		1 aryballos
Epiktetos	Epiktetos	1 plate
Epigenes	Eretria Painter	1 kantharos
Erginos	Aristophanes	2 kylikes
Euergides	Euergides Painter	9 kylikes
	prob. Euergides Painter	1 kylix
	Unattributed	2 kylikes
Euphamos	Unattributed	1 fragment
Euphronios	Onesimos	9 kylikes
	manner of Onesimos	2 kylikes
	near Onesimos (possibly)	2 kylikes
	Pistoxenos Painter	3 kylikes
Euxitheos	Oltos	2 kylikes and 1 amphora
	Euphronios	2 calyx-kraters
Gales	Gales Painter	2 lekythoi
Gaurion	Unattributed	3 pyxides
Gorgos	Berlin Painter	1 kylix
Hegesiboulos	Hegesiboulos Painter	1 kylix
	near Sotades Painter	1 stemless cup
Hermaios	Hermaios Painter	3 kylikes
	prob. Hermaios Painter	1 kylix
Hieron	Makron	3 skyphoi and 30 kylikes
	Telephos Painter	2 kylikes
	Amphitrite Painter	1 kantharos
	Unattributed	7 kylikes and 1 skyphos
Hilinos	Psiax	2 alabastra
Hischylos*	Hischylos Painter	1 kylix
	Epiktetos	6 kylikes
	prob. Epiktetos	1 kylix
	Pheidippos	3 kylikes
	Painter of Cambridge	
	Hischylos	1 kylix
	Unattributed	2 kylikes
Kachrylion	Hermaios Painter	7 kylikes
	prob. Hermaios Painter	1 kylix
	Oltos	7 kylikes
	Euphronios	2 kylikes
	Thalia Painter	2 kylikes
	Painter of Louvre G 36	2 kylikes
	Unattributed	8 kylikes and 1 plate
Kalliades	Douris	1 kylix
Kallis	Unattributed	1 small pot
Kleophrades,	Kleophrades Painter	1 kylix
son of Amasis	Douris	1 kylix

POTTER'S NAME	ASSOCIATION	ITEMS
Meidias	Meidias Painter	1 hydria
Megakles	Pistoxenos Painter	1 pyxis
Menon	Psiax	1 amphora
Midas	Unattributed	1 head vase
Mikion	Mikion Painter	2 lekanides
	Unattributed	1 plaque
Myson	Myson	1 column-krater
Nikias	Nikias Painter	1 bell-krater
Nikosthenes*	Nikosthenes Painter	1 skyphoid, 1 kantharos and 1 pyxis
	Oltos	1 kyathos
	Epiktetos	1 kylix and 1 kantharos
	Group of Louvre F 125	2 kylikes
	Unattributed	1 kantharos
Oreibelos	Deepdene Painter	1 volute-krater
Paidikos**	Euergides Painter	2 kylikes
	manner of Euergides Painter	5 kylikes
	Painter of Bologna 433	1 kylix
	Unattributed	8 alabastra and 6 kylikes
	Paidikos (?)	1 kylix
Pamphaios*	Oltos	1 Nikosthenic amphora, 1 neck-amphora and 1 stamnos
	Epiktetos	3 kylikes
	Nikosthenes Painter	10 kylikes
	Unattributed	23 kylikes
Pasiades***	Pasiades Painter	2 white alabastra
	Group of Paidikos Alabastra	2 white alabastra
	Painter of Frankfort Acorn	1 (shape ?)
	Unattributed	1 white alabastron
Phintias	Unattributed	2 aryballoi and 2 kylikes
Phintias (II)	Painter of the Frankfort Acorn	1 lekythos
Pistoxenos	Pistoxenos Painter	1 skyphos
	Syriskos Painter	2 skyphoi
	Epiktetos	1 skyphos
	PS Painter	2 skyphoi
	Unattributed	1 skyphos and 1 kylix
Proklees	Unattributed	1 aryballos
Python	Douris	3 kylikes
	Epiktetos	1 kylix
Sikanos	near Oltos	1 stemmed plate
Soklees****	near Paseas	1 plate

POTTER'S NAME	ASSOCIATION	ITEMS
Sosias	Sosias Painter	1 kylix
	Unattributed	1 standlet
Sotades	Sotades Painter	2 kylikes and 1 kantharos
	Unattributed	2 phialai, 3 rhyta and 1 fragment
Syriskos	Syriskos Painter	1 astragalos
Tleson*	Oltos	1 kylix
Xenophantos	Xenophantos Painter	2 squat lekythoi
Xenotimos	Xenotimos Painter	1 stemless kylix

* Also a potter of black-figured items.
** May be the same as Pasiades.
*** May be the same as Paidikos.
**** The signature may not be genuine; if it is, this may be the Soklees who potted five black-figured cups.

APPENDIX IV

KALOS AND KALÉ NAMES

Again, I am indebted to Sir John D. Beazley for the love names included in this appendix. Beazley's *Attic Red-figure Vase Painter,* Appendix IV (as amended by his *Paralipomena*), lists and describes the vases on which each name appears.

In the following lists, I have indicated uncertainties as follows: (1) a question mark before the love name indicates that it is not certain that it really is a love name (i.e., it might be some other type of inscription); (2) a question mark after the love name indicates that the spelling of the name is uncertain; (3) brackets are used to indicate letters supplied, but presumably correct.

KALOS (MASCULINE) NAMES

Kalos Name	Associated Painter(s) and/or Comments
Agasias	Unattributed
Agasikrates	Unattributed
Aischines	Aischines P.
Aisimides	Unattributed—vague resemblance to early Onesimos
Akestor	Salting P.
Akestorides	Akestorides P. (without *kalos*)
	Oionokles P.
	Timocrates P.
	Makron (partial name might be Akestorides)
Alexomenos	Unattributed—Early Classic
Alkaios	Achilles P.
Alkibiades	Briseis P.—doubtful that inscription is genuine
Alkimachos, son of Epichares	Alkimachos P.
	Timocrates P.
	Vouni P.
	Manner of early Achilles P. possibly Proto-Panaetian Group. Partial inscription in manner of Pistoxenos Painter

Kalos Name	Associated Painter(s) and/or Comments
Alkimachos (II)	Chicago P.
	Epimedes P.
	Lykaon P.
	Group of Polygnotos (but rather apart from this group)
Alkimachos (III?)	Kalliope P.
	Eretria P. (without *kalos*)
Alkimedes, son of Aischylides	Achilles P.
Alkmeon	Brygos P.
	Berlin P.
Antias	Euphronios
	Smikros
	Colmar P. (probably)
	Proto-Panaetian Group (not a *kalos* name)
Antimachos	Ambrosios P. (partial inscription)
	Proto-Panaetian Group (without *kalos*)
	Near the Scheurleer P.
Antiphanes	Makron (Tag-kallistos)
	Plus an earlier Antiphanes: Oltos
Antiphon	Antiphon P.
Apollodoros	Argos P. (signature fragmental)
Archinos (I)	Dutuit P.
Archinos (II)	P. of London E 777
Aristagoras	Magnoncourt P.
	Douris
	Makron (misspelled)
Aristarchos	Onesimos
	Antiphon P.
Aristeides	Eucharides P.
Aristoleon	Unattributed
Aristomenes	Aristomenes P.
Ariston	Syriskos P.
Athenodotos	Proto-Panaetian Group
	Onesimos
	Peithinos
	Colmar P.
	Akin to Douris
?Autoboulos	Oltos
Automenes	Oltos
Axiopeithes, son of Alkimachos	Achilles P. (patronymic on 4 items)
	Lykaon P. (patronymic not shown)
?[B]oukolos	Onesimos
Brachas	Related to Psiax
Chairestratos	Douris
Chairias (I)	Chairias P.
	Phintias

Kalos Name	Associated Painter(s) and/or Comments
Chairias (I)	P. of Agora Chairias Cups
	Somewhat in style of Thalia P.
	Somewhat in style of Eucharides P.
Chairias (II)	Syriskos P.
Chairippos (I)	Chairippos P.
	Epiktetos
Chairippos (II)	P. of London D 15
Chairis	Chicago P.
Charmaios	Related to Charmides P.
Charmides	Charmides P.
	Providence P.
	Nikon P.
	Dresden P.
	P. of Yale Lekythos (probably by this painter)
	Cat and Dog P.
	Early Classical follower of Douris
Charops	Charops P.
	Bowdoin Eye P.
Chilon	Oltos
?Chion	Oltos
Damas	Argos P.
	Brygos P.
	Plus another Damas without *kalos* by
	Euthymides
Dikaios	Dikaios P.
Dikaios (II)	Meidias P.
Diogenes	Diogenes P.
	Douris
	Foundry P.
	Antiphon P.
	Syriskos P.
Diokles	Tithonos P.
Dion	Dwarf P.
	Sabouroff P.
	P. of Munich 2363
Dioxippos	Oltos
Diphilos (I)	Brygos P. (tag-*kalos*)
Diphilos (II), son of	
Melanopos	Achilles P. (patronymic on 12 items,
	omitted on 2)
	P. of Athens 12789 (patronymic omitted)
	Kraipale P. (appears without *kalos*)
Diphilos (III)	Unattributed
Dorotheos	Epeleios P.
	Proto-Panaetian Group (tag-*kalos*)
	Near the Scheurleer P.
	Paseas (appears without *kalos*)
	Oltos (appears without *kalos*)

Kalos Name	Associated Painter(s) and/or Comments
Dromippos, son of Dromokleides	Achilles P. (all items add patronymic)
?Elaion	Probably should be Euaion
Elpinikos	Elpinikos P.
Epeleios	Epeleios P.
Epidromos	Epidromos P.
	Salting P.
	Kiss P.
	Proto-Panaetian Group (Onesimos ?)
	Paseas (probably, on a fragment)
Epilykos	Skythes
	Pedieus P.
	Near the Carpenter Painter
	Phintias (apparently not a *kalos* name)
Epimedes	Epimedes P.
[E]rinos	Unattributed
Erothemis	Onesimos
Euaion, son of Aischylos	Euaion P.
	Providence P. (one without patronymic)
	Lykaon P.
	Achilles P. (without patronymic)
	Phiale P. (one without patronymic)
Eualkides	Smikros
Eualkos	Spreckels P.
Eucharides	Eucharides P.
	Triptolemos P. (partial inscription)
Eun[ikos]	Unattributed mid 5th century
	Plus a later Eunikos by Group of Polygnotos
Euryptolemos	Apollodoros
Euthyd[ikos]	Unattributed
Ganymedes	Meidias P.
Glaukon, son of Leagros	Pistoxenos P.
	Tarquinia P.
	Providence P. (patronymic on one item)
	Nikon P.
	P. of Yale Lekythos
	Timokrates P. (patronymic added)
	Cat and Dog P.
	(Note: The patronymic appears only on 5 items, some unattributed)
Glaukytes	Apparently a partial erasure and substitution for Megakles on a plaque related to Euthymides
Hegeleos	Achilles P.
Hektor	Ashby P. (possibly)
	Recalls Eleusis P. and Proto-Panaetian Group

Kalos Name	Associated Painter(s) and/or Comments
Herias	Hypsis
?Herias?	Unattributed
?Hermo. . .	Unattributed
Hermogenes	Douris
Hestiaios	Manner of Euthymedes
Hiketes	Makron
	Painter of Philadelphia 2449
	Douris
Hilaron	Oionokles P.
Hipparchos	Epiktetos
	Euergides P.
	Group of Paidikos Alabastra
	Charops P.
	Bonn P. (without *kalos*)
Hippodamas	Makron
	Douris
Hippokrates	Psiax (on black-figure side of bilingual vase)
Hippolochos	Syriskos P.
[Hip]pome[don]	Recalls Hermaios P.
Hippon (I)	Manner of the Epeleios P.
Hippon (II)	Providence P.
	Charmides P.
	Dresden P.
	Myson
	Near the Pan P.
	Somewhat recalls Nikon P.
Hippoxenos	Providence P.
Hygiainon	Achilles P.
Iasimachos	Providence P.
Isarchos	Epeleios P.
Isthmodoros	Euaichme P.
Kachrylion	Thalia P.
Kalliades	Akin to Charmides P.
Kallias (I)	Oionokles P.
	Nikon P.
	Related to Charmides P.
	Plus an earlier Kallias without *kalos* by the Ambrosios P.
Kallias (II)	Eretria P.
	Group of Polygnotos
	Manner of Kleophon P.
Kallikles	Providence P.
	Nikon P.
	Dresden P.
Kallimachos	Douris
?Kallon	Unattributed
Karton	Copenhagen P.

Kalos Name	Associated Painter(s) and/or Comments
Karystios	Psiax
?Kench[ros]	Unattributed
Kephisophon	Proto-Panaetian Group (tag-*kalos*)
Kleinias, son of	
Pedieus	Alkimachos P.
	Achilles P.
	Close to the Dish P. (without *kalos*)
Kleomelos	Kleomelos P.
Kleophon	Kleophon P.
Klinias	Ambrosios P. (probably not *kalos* name)
Krates	Skythes
	Berlin P.
	Proto-Panaetian Group
Kytinos	Unattributed
Labotos	Unattributed
Lacheas	Tyszkiewicz P.
Laches	Antiphon P.
Leagros	Euphronios
	Phintias
	Euthymides
	Eleusis P.
	Proto-Panaetian Group
	Onesimos
	Colmar P.
	Thalia P.
	Kiss P.
	Myson
	Plus numerous unassigned items
Leosthenes	Douris
Lichas, son of	
Samieus	Telephos P.
	P. of Munich SL 477
	Alkimachos P.
	P. of Athens 1826
	Achilles P. (patronymic given on one item)
	Plus one unattributed item
	Near Timokrates P.
Liteus	Recalls the Alkimachos P.
Lyandros	Lyandros P.
Lykos	Onesimos
	Antiphon P.
	Manner of Tarquinia P.
	Copenhagen P. (probaby same Lykos)
	Tryptolemos P. (probably same Lykos)
	Foundry P.
	Plus another Lykos, possibly by the Flying Angel P.

Kalos Name	Associated Painter(s) and/or Comments
Lykos	The name appears also probably for an athlete by Euphronios
	Also on an item related to Phintias
Lyseas	Terpaulos P.
Lysikles	Thaliarchos P.
Lysis	Colmar P.
	Antiphon P.
	Cage P.
	Pistoxenos P.
Megakles (I)	Phintias
	Euthymides
Megakles (II)	Kleophon P.
	Orestes P.
	Group of Polygnotos
Melas	Euphronios
Meletos	Achilles P. (early)
Melieus	Goluchow P.
Memmnon	Chelis P.
Memnon	Oltos
M[e]nis	Pheidippos
Menon	Douris
Me. . .tos	Unattributed-early Classic
Mikion	Unattributed
Milon	Oltos
Miltiades	Paseas
?Molpis	Oltos
Nausistratos	Unattributed
?Nikodemos	Polygnotos
Nikomas	Polygnotos
Nikon (I)	Oltos
	Name Nikon also occurs on items by Myson and Makron—however is a fourth Nikon
Nikon (II)	Nikon P.
	Providence P.
	Villa Giulia P.
	Euaion P.
	Recalls Alkimachos P.
Nikon (III)	Polion
Nikondas	Manner of Alkimachos P.
Nikostratos	Berlin P.
	Hephaisteion P.
	Triptolemos P.
	Antiphon P.
	Copenhagen P. (*kalos* missing—covered by by paint?)
Nikoxenos	Nikoxenos P.
Oionokles	Oionokles P.

Kalos Name	Associated Painter(s) and/or Comments
Olympichos	Syriskos P.
Olympiadoros	Proto-Panaetian Group
	Related to Phintias
Pammachos	Apollodoros
Panaitios	Proto-Panaetian Group
	Onesimos
	Colmar P.
	Douris
	Magnoncourt P.
Pausimachos	Unattributed
Pedieus	Pedieus P.
	Plus one unattributed item
Phaidimos	Thanatos P.
?Phaidri[as]	Magnoncourt P.
Phainippos	Unattributed
Phanos	P. of London D 15
[Ph]ei[d]iades	Smikros
Pheidon	Near Scheurleer P.
Philiades	Euphronios
Philokomos	Euergides P.
Philon	Brygos P. (tag-*kalos*)
	Triptolemos P. (without *kalos*)
	Phintias (without *kalos*)
Pistoxenos, son of	
Aresandros	Achilles P.
Pithon	Nikoxenos P.
?Polemainetos?	Group of Polygnotos
Polydemos	Makron
Polyeuktos	Following of Douris—early Classical
Polyphrasmon	Douris
Praxiteles	Makron
Psolon	Period of Dinos P.
Pythaios	Douris
Pythodelos	Kraipale P.
	Plus an earlier Pythodelos by Ambrosios P.
Pythodoros	(Graffito)
Pythokles	Pythokles P.
Sibyrtios	Unattributed—late Sixth Century
Sikinos	Unattributed
Simiades	Oltos
Smikrion	Psiax
Smikros	Unattributed
?Smikros	Oltos
Smikythos	Euphronios
	Oltos (without *kalos*)
	Phintias (without *kalos*)
	Euthymides (without *kalos*)

Kalos Name	Associated Painter(s) and/or Comments
Sokrates	Berlin P.
?Solon	Oltos
Sophanes	Trophy P.
	Following of Douris—early Classical
Sostratos	Phintias
Stesagoras	Recalls Salting P.
Stysippos	Oltos
Teisias	Charmides P.
Thaliarchos	Thaliarchos P.
Theodoros	Epeleios P.
Therikles	Unattributed (Graffito)
Thespieus	Unattributed (Graffito)
Timarchos	Syriskos P.
Timodemos	Unattributed—early Classic
Timokrates	Timokrates P.
	Recalls Alkimachos P.
Timonides	Providence P.
	Nikon P. (may be same misspelled)
Timoxenos	Charmides P.
	Dresden P.
	Nikon P.
Tlempolemos	Euergides P.
	Phintias
Tleson	Ambrosios P.
Trageas	P. of Berlin 2268
Xanthes (I)	Ambrosios P.
Xanthes (II)	Nikon P.
Xenon (I)	Euphronios
Xenon (II)	Kodros P.

KALÉ (Feminine) NAMES

Kalé Name	Associated Painter(s) and/or Comments
Aphrodesia	Chairippos P. Comparable to work of Painter of Wurzburg 517 Plus probably another Aphrodesia by Makron
Archedike	Sabouroff P.
Epicharis	Meidias P.
Epilyke	Unattributed
Erosanthe	Comparable to work of the Painter of Wurzburg 517
Hediste	Group of Polygnotos
Heras	Nikon P. Penthesileia P. Wedding P. Pistoxenos P. Splanchnopt P.
Kleitagora	Group of Polygnotos
Kleophonis	Group of Polygnotos
Louda (or Lyda)	Onesimos
?Melitta	Makron
Myia?	Unattributed
Myrrhinske	Meidias P.
Naukleia	Makron
Nikophile	Brygos P.
Oinanthe	Oinanthe P.
Pantoxena	Pantoxena P.
Rhodo?	Unattributed third quarter of fifth century
Rhodopis	Makron
Zephyria	Unattributed (tag-*kale*)

APPENDIX V

STATISTICAL SUMMARY

There were, of course, many painters and potters whose names are not known and who have not been given names by archaeologists. Sir John D. Beazley in his *Attic Red-figure Vase Painters,* as amended by his *Paralipomena,* lists some 770 painters and groups to whom two or more items are attributed as well as a few who are known by only one signed item. Other authorities have given names to additional painters not listed in Beazley's works. It is, however, interesting to summarize the number of painters, potters, *kalos* and *kalé* names listed in Beazley's works as indicative of the number of recognized artists, the number of those who signed their works, and their love name inscriptions. Table 1 summarizes this information.

TABLE 1: The Number of Painters, Potters, *Kalos*, and *Kalé* Names, ca. 530-320 B.C., Identified by Beazley

Artists/Inscriptions	Archaic Period		Classical Period		Fifth Century B.C.	Fourth Century B.C.	Other	Total
	Early	Late	Early	Late				
	← ← ← ← ← ← ← ← ← ← ← ← Number Identified ← ← ← ← ← ← ← ← ← ← ← →							
Identified painters and groups	75	94	190	205	92	114	–	770
Painters who signed their works	15	7	2	4	2	–	–	30
Potters who signed their works	23	7	4	2	5	1	10[a]	52
Different *kalos* names	72	59	41	31	2	–	33[b]	238[c]
Different *kalé* names	–	7	3	5	2	–	3[b]	20[c]

[a]Includes 2 potters who worked from the early Archaic into the early Classical period, 1 potter who worked throughout the Archaic period, 2 potters who overlapped from the late Archaic period into the early Classical period, and 5 potters for whom dates are not available.

[b]Includes names found on unattributed and not clearly dateable items.

[c]Totals differ from Appendix IV due to repetition of names in different periods.

GLOSSARY OF TERMS

(Not already explained in the text)

ALABASTRON. A small vase, elongated with a narrow neck, without handles, but sometimes with string holes or lugs; size about 7–20 cm. (3–8 inches); used as a perfume container.

ANIMAL STYLE. A style of painting in which animals predominate.

APOTROPAIC. A term used for objects that supposedly avert evil.

ARCHAIC PERIOD. ca. 700–480 B.C.

ARYBALLOS. A rounded oil bottle with a narrow neck; size 5–13 cm. (2–5 inches); commonly used by athletes at bath.

ASKOS. A small flask with a circular body wider than high with a convex top and an arched handle reaching from one side across the top to a spout on the other side; size 5–15 cm. (2–6 inches); used for containing oil.

ASTRAGALOS. An odd shape in the form of a knuckle-bone.

CHITON. A light-weight sleeved tunic, usually of linen, worn by women.

CHOUS. A very squat type of oinochoe.

CLASSICAL PERIOD. ca. 480–323 B.C. (for vase painting, usually divided into classical [480–420 B.C.], late fifth century, and fourth century.

DINOS. See LEBES.

ECHINUS. A convex molding.

ENGOBE. See SLIP.

EPINETRON. See ONOS.

GEOMETRIC PERIOD. ca. 900–700 B.C.

HELLENISTIC PERIOD. ca. 323–27 B.C.

HIMATION. A heavy mantle or cloak, usually of wool.

HUMAN STYLE. A style of painting in which human figures predominate.

INCISION. Engraving with a sharp point.

KANTHAROS. A deep cup with two tall vertical handles; the base may be low or pedestal and the cup may be stemmed or unstemmed.

KYATHOS. A ladle in the form of a deep cup with one tall vertical handle.

LEBES. A deep round bowl.

LEKANIS. A flat bowl with a cover, two handles set horizontally and a rim to receive the lid.

OBVERSE. (opposite of reverse) side of vase with the main picture.

OINOCHOE. A jug or pitcher with one vertical handle at the back; size varied, usually about 30 cm. (12 inches); used for pouring wine.

OLPE. A slender oinochoe with a sagging belly.

ONOS. A special shape designed to fit over knee and thigh, used for roughening thread after spinning.

PEPLOS. A heavy sleeveless garment, usually of wool, worn by women.

PHIALE. A low, stemless, shallow cup without handles, used for drinking and pouring libations; often it had a central boss.

PROTO-ATTIC PERIOD. ca. 710–610 B.C.

PROTOGEOMETRIC PERIOD. ca. 1050–900 B.C.

PSYKTER. Similar in shape to an amphora, but without handles; or a double-walled type of amphora with a spout; used for cooling wine.

PYXIS. A small round box, usually without handles; usually about 10 cm. (4 inches) across; used to hold cosmetics or trinkets.

RESERVED. Left in the color of the clay.

REVERSE. See OBVERSE.

RHYTON. A deep horn-shaped cup or a cup in the form of an animal's head.

SEMI-OUTLINE. Partly black silhouette and partly outline.

SKYPHOS. A deep cup with two horizontal handles, no stem and a low or pedestal base (also known as a kotyle).

SLIP. A liquid clay applied as a coating on a vase prior to firing.

TAG KALOS. Names of figures depicted to which *kalos* has been attached.

TONDO. A disk or circular picture inside a kylix.

TORUS. A convex molding.

BIBLIOGRAPHY

Arias, P.E. and Hirmer, M., *A History of Greek Vase Painting*, translated and revised by B.B. Shefton, London, Thames and Hudson, 1962. A large volume profusely illustrated with textual coverage of major artists.

Beazley, J.D. and Ashmole, Bernard, *Greek Sculpture and Painting to the End of the Hellenistic Period*, Cambridge, University Press, 1932.

Beazley, Sir John Davidson, "Attic Black-figure: A Sketch," *Proceedings of the British Academy*, Vol. XIV, London, Humphrey Milford Amen House, E.C., Oxford, University of Oxford Press, 1930. A lecture delivered in 1928.

_____, *Attic Black-figure Vase Painters*, Oxford, Clarendon Press, 1956. The authoritative work on Attic black-figure painters, the works attributed to them, groups of items, classes of items, potters' names, love names, etc.

_____, *Attic Red-figured Vases in American Museums*, Cambridge, Harvard University Press, 1918. Interesting, though now outdated.

_____, *Attic Red-figure Vase Painters*, Oxford, Clarendon Press, 1942. Now replaced by the following.

_____, *Attic Red-figure Vase Painters*, Oxford, Clarendon Press, 1963, Vols. I-III. The authoritative work on Attic red-figure painters and the works attributed to them, groups of items, classes of items, potters' names, love names, etc.

_____, *Attic White Lekythoi*, London, Oxford University Press, Humphrey Milford, 1938 (The William Henry Charlton Memorial Lecture, Nov. 1937). A summary of shapes, decoration, subjects, and styles.

_____, *Paralipomena: Additions to Attic Black-figure Vase Painters and to Attic Red-figure Vase Painters*, 2nd ed., Oxford, Clarendon Press, 1971. This last work by Sir John D. Beazley brings his former two classic works up-to-date.

_____, "Potter and Painter in Ancient Athens," *Proceedings of the British Academy*, Vol. XXX, London, Geoffrey Cumberlege Amen House, E.C. 4, 1946. A lecture delivered to the Joint Meeting of Classical Societies at Oxford in 1942, revised and expanded. An interesting, brief (43 pages) discussion of the works of potters and painters and how they worked.

_____, *The Development of Attic Black-figure*, Sather Classical Lecture, Vol. 24, Berkeley and Los Angeles, University of California Press. 1951. An excellent summary of the subject.

Boardman, John, *Greek Art*, New York, Washington, Frederick A. Praeger, Publishers, 1964 (reprinted 1965). One of the Praeger World of Art Paperbacks; devoted to Greek art in all forms.

Bothmer, Dietrich von, "Andokides the Potter and the Andokides Painter," *Bulletin*, New York, N.Y. The Metropolitan Museum of Art, February, 1966.

_____, "Greek Vase Painting," *Bulletin*, New York, The Metropolitan Museum of Art, Fall, 1972.

Carpenter, Rhys, *Greek Art: A Study of the Formal Evolution of Style,* Philadelphia, University of Pennsylvania Press, 1962. See especially pages 85-91 on symmetry of Greek vases.

Caskey, L.D., *Geometry of Greek Vases,* Boston, Museum of Fine Arts, 1922, (Communications to the Trustees V). An attempt to provide evidence from Attic black-figured and red-figured pottery in the Boston Museum of Fine Arts in support of Jay Hambidge's theory that Greek artistic design was based on geometric principles.

Cook, R.M., *Greek Painted Pottery,* London, Methuen and Co. Ltd., 1960. A readable and comprehensive survey of Greek painted pottery from the Protogeometric Period to the Hellenistic Period, with special sections on shapes, techniques, inscriptions, potting, the history of the study of vase painting, etc.

Devambez, Pierre, *Greek Painting,* New York, The Viking Press, 1962. One of the Compass History of Art series. Well illustrated with a brief text dealing primarily with Greek vase painting, but covering painting from Cretan to Roman times.

Fairbanks, Arthur, *Athenian Lekythoi with Outline Drawing in Glaze Varnish on a White Ground,* New York, Macmillan Co., 1907. (University of Michigan Studies—Humanistic Series, Vol. VI). See below.

————, *Athenian Lekythoi with Outline Drawing in Matt Color on a White Ground,* New York, Macmillan Co., 1914, (University of Michigan Studies—Humanistic Series, Vol. VII). These two volumes by Fairbanks constitute an early study of white lekythoi, but resulted in a too credulous and too methodical cataloguing.

Farnsworth, Marie and Wisely, Harriet, "Fifth Century Intentional Red Glaze," *American Journal of Archaeology* 62 (1958), pp. 165-173, Plate 36 and color plate.

Folsom, Robert S., *Attic Black-figured Pottery,* Park Ridge, N.J., Noyes Press, 1975. A summary of the development of the black figure technique from the late seventh century B.C. to mid-fifth century B.C.

————, *Handbook of Greek Pottery: A Guide for Amateurs,* London, Faber and Faber, 1967. A concise summary of Greek pottery from the Protogeometric to the Hellenistic Period.

Hambidge, Jay, *Dynamic Symmetry—The Greek Vase,* New Haven, Yale University Press, 1948 Ed. Excellent for cross-sections of Greek vases showing symmetry of forms.

Hereford, Mary A.B., *A Handbook of Greek Vase Painting,* London, University of Manchester Press, Longmans Green & Co., 1919. An historical account of Greek vases from the Cretan period to the late Italiote with chapters on potters, painters, shapes, and uses—now outdated.

Hoppin, Joseph Clark, *A Handbook of Attic Red-figured Vases,* Cambridge, Harvard University Press, 1919. Arranged alphabetically by painters, listing items then attributed to each, with descriptions, sketches, and photographs. Though outdated, it is useful as a quick reference to styles of the various painters.

211

Lane, Arthur, *Greek Pottery*, London, Faber and Faber, 1963. A brief, but well-illustrated and concise summary of Greek pottery from the Protogeometric to the Hellenistic Period.

Noble, Joseph Veach, *The Techniques of Painted Attic Pottery*, New York, Watson-Guptill Publishers and the Metropolitan Museum of Art, 1965. A basic work, extremely readable and profusely illustrated.

Pfuhl, Ernst, *Malerei und Zeichnung der Griechen*, Munich, F. Bruckmann A.G., 1923. A massive work.

———, *Masterpieces of Greek Drawing and Painting*, translated by J.D. Beazley, New York, Macmillan Co., 1926. Contains selections from the above to present a collection of masterpieces in photographs.

Richter, Gisela M.A., *A Handbook of Greek Art*, London, The Phaidon Press, 1960. (especially pp. 327-346). An excellent summary of Attic red-figure in a book on Greek art in general.

———, *Attic Red Figured Vases—A Survey*, New Haven, Yale University Press, 1958. An excellent source in popular form.

———, *Red Figured Athenian Vases in the Metropolitan Museum of Art*, New Haven, Yale University Press, 1936, 2 vols. (Vol. I text and Vol. II drawings and photographs). Updated by Miss Richter's *Survey* listed above.

———, and Milne, Marjorie J., *Shapes and Names of Athenian Vases*, New York, Metropolitan Museum of Art, 1935. The definitive work on the subject.

———, *The Craft of Athenian Pottery*, New Haven, Yale University Press, 1923. Interesting, but now out of date (See Noble, J.V. above).

Robertson, Martin, *Greek Painting*, Geneva, Skira, 1959. A well-illustrated survey of Greek painting with special emphasis on painted pottery.

Schoder, Raymond V., *Masterpieces of Greek Art*, London, Studio Books, undated. Devoted to all ancient Greek art forms. This book contains some excellent illustrations of red-figured vases.

Vermeule, Emily, "A Love Scene by the 'Panaitios Painter'," *American Journal of Archaeology*, Volume 71, No. 3, July, 1967.

Walters, H.B., *History of Ancient Pottery*, 3 volumes, New York, Charles Scribner's Sons, 1905. A monumental work covering Greek pottery in general, sites, discovery, uses of clay, shapes, history, subjects portrayed, etc., plus Italian vases.

Webster, T.B.L., *Potter and Patron in Classical Athens*, London, Methuen and Co., 1972. As indicated by the title, this is a study of the influence of buyers on pottery production.

214